Cats' Company

By Ann Walker

Cats' Company

ISBN 1 898307 32 6

First published in Australia 1985
This edition published 1995

Cover design by Daryth Bastin

Published by:

Capall Bann Publishing
Freshfields
Chieveley
Berks
RG16 8TF

Contents

To the memory of Tiny, best loved of all my company of cats.

Acknowledgements

My particular thanks to Letty Gregory for sharing with me, and giving me permission to use, some of her own treasury of cat stories: 'Why', 'Prudence', 'Carlotta' and 'The Fairy Prince'.

To Patrick York-Moore for permission to use the poem 'Acceptance' by my good friend the late June York-Moore.

To Neville Drury for permission to use material on Rosaleen Norton.

And to the many friends who have so generously shared with me their own particular experiences of cats' company.

Chapter 1
The Lion on the Mat

Cats - you either love 'em or you hate 'em; and the curious thing is that people in both camps give exactly the same reasons for their feelings! Paradoxical, yes, but no more so than the cat herself - the lion on the mat.

Domesticated since time immemorial, the cat is the least domesticated of all animals. She has learned to live with man - or man has learned to live with her, sharing his home and his lifestyle every bit as closely as with the dog. Unlike the dog, however, she has not bartered her personal sovereignty for that privilege.

Cats can be bred and traded, they can even be caged, but no-one can make a cat do anything It does not already have some desire to do. While there are countless ways in which the dog has been taught to serve man, the only record we have - right down the ages - of cats doing anything of the kind comes to us from pre-Christian times and the great civilisations of the Pharaohs. - Ancient Egyptian papyrus paintings show cats on leashes in the flat-bottomed boats of waterfowl hunters amongst the reedy waters of the Nile. The cats, apparently, were persuaded to retrieve the fowl from the water - a remarkable achievement of persuasion on the part of the Egyptians considering the cat's natural aversion to water!

This working relationship between cat and man, however, is unique in both their histories. To the Ancient Egyptians the cat, known as Bast or Pasht, was the most sacred of their many animal gods. She was the beloved companion of Ra himself, the great sun god, and represented the many female aspects of the god. In another form she was worshipped as Isis, the moon-goddess.

The cat, as we all know, has wonderful eyes with remarkable night vision. It was this quality that linked her with the moon. The Egyptians believed that when the sun, Ra, set at night he journeyed through the gloom of the underworld until morning; the moon, Isis, pierced the darkness on his behalf. So the cat could pierce the darkness, even that of the underworld through which the soul must travel on its journey to Paradise after death. Pious Egyptians made sure they were buried with cat effigies, amulets or charms to help them on their way.

When the cat herself died, she was mummified and burled with great ceremony. H.C. Brooke described this in his poem 'Lines to an Abyssinian Cat', written in 1925:

> -Then wast thou divine!
> Thou didst recline on Pharaoh's golden throne;
> And when thy time upon this earth was o'er -
> And mighty Pharaoh, too, must pass away,
> Ptah-Seker-Asar* having called ye hence -
> Then cunning workmen wrapped thy slender form
> In choicest swaddling cloths, with spices rare,
> And, jewel-decked thou shared'st the Pharaoh's tomb.

*The triune god of the resurrection.

The cat has many facets to her personality. The Ancient Egyptian and the modern cat lover would both agree that one of these is the ruthless hunter, the 'tearer and render'. The Egyptian goddess Sekhmet represented this side of her and was often portrayed as a lion-headed, rather than a cat-headed goddess. She was often shown In old papyrus paintings as the figure of a woman with a cat's or lion's head and her feet upon a serpent or as slaying~ a serpent with a sword.

The earliest known portrait depicting the cat as a goddess dates from approximately 3000 BC. The cult of the cat began about then and remained at its height for some 2000 years. It has never quite died - there are many people today who avow that they adore cats. Those who claim to dislike cats do so for exactly the same reasons as their devotees adore them - they recognise the inherent feeling of superiority in the cat's make-up and are repelled by it.

The Egyptians, in spite of their mysticism and apparent preoccupation with death and the afterlife in their religion, were also very practical people and they were quick to recognise the value of their cat-goddess in her aspect of Sekhmet, the tearer and render, in protecting their grain stores from the ravages of rodents.

This indeed must have been the golden era for Puss. She never, before or since, had it quite so good. Cats were protected by law, and to kill one was a crime punishable by death. Ordinary household cats were treated with the greatest possible respect. Often bejewelled, they shared their owners' dishes; when sick they were tended with care and when dead buried with reverence, pomp and ceremony. indeed, upon its death the cat's human family would shave off their eyebrows as a symbol of mourning, wrap the body in a linen sheet and carry it, amid great lamentation, to the house of the embalmer where it was treated with drugs and spices, placed in a specially made case and finally laid to rest in the sacred vaults. Cat funerals were sumptuous affairs, accompanied by much beating of breasts and cymbals, particularly if the deceased happened to have been one of the special temple cats. If the family could possibly afford it the mummified body was dispatched to Bubastis, the city sacred to the great cat-goddess Pasht herself. Here, in the late nineteenth century, close by the site of the ancient city, a huge cat cemetery was accidentally discovered. Hundreds of thousands of pathetic little corpses, carefully preserved by the embalmer's skill, were found ranged neatly on shelves.

Some were stolen, some destroyed, many were seized on by dealers to sell to tourists. Still they remained there in their thousands until an Alexandrian speculator saw a way to turn them into money by offering them for sale as fertiliser! In 1890 a cargo of 180,000 arrived in Liverpool to be sold by auction. They made £3.13s.9d. a ton. What a sad and inglorious end to so much reverence, skill, and love. As a final touch of bathos the auctioneer used one as a hammer!

The embalming and elaborate funerals accorded to cats were based on the Egyptian belief in their immortality and on the idea that it was essential to preserve the physical body ready for the soul when the animal wanted to return.

Herodotus, the historian, who travelled in Egypt around 450 BC, gave us a vivid description of the sacred city of Bubastis and the temple of Pasht which stood in the centre of the city - virtually on an island, he tells us, for it was surrounded by canals from the Nile which were overhung by trees. The temple itself was built of red granite in the form of a square. A grove of tall trees in the centre surrounded a shrine in which stood the statue of the cat-goddess.

Herodotus also records how the Persian army once won a victory over the Egyptians by throwing live cats over the city walls. The defending Egyptian soldiers, rather than risk injuring these animals which they held as sacred and moreover believed to be divine, allowed the city to be captured.

The Egyptians of the Pharaohs were not alone in suspecting the cat of something more than earthly nature. Right down the ages she has been credited with supernatural powers. Her detractors have linked her with the dark side, the occult, but many, like the famous artist Rosaleen Norton, recognised their spiritual qualities.

Rosaleen Norton, who died in 1979, was often referred to as 'The Witch of Kings Cross'. True to the public idea of a witch, she lived in virtual seclusion with her cats for the last years of her life, her strange paintings of supernatural deities were often a blend of the human and the animal. She had a great empathy for animals, for she felt they had retained their integrity more than humans, and was particularly devoted to cats, who she believed could operate in waking consciousness and on the astral plane at the same time and had a spiritual sensitivity which she considered to be lacking in mankind as a whole,

Perhaps she and the Egyptians were right - the somnolent cat apparently dozing its days away by the hearth or in the warmth of the sun is not actually there at all but away on some strange astral sphere of existence. The idea is not hard to believe when you live with a cat, or cats, and try to understand the paradox that is Puss, or Pasht.

Anyone who claims to understand cats is either a liar and a self-deluding one at that - or a genius. As I don't wish to be thought the former and have no claims to be the latter, I had better confess here and now that I do not understand cats. To me they are an enigma, a fascinating mystery - this in spite of the fact that, to a lesser or greater extent, my journey through life has been in cats' company!

Most mysterious of all the cats travelling with me at the present time is Sheba. Beautiful, aloof, apparently helpless Sheba. There is a whole area of her life I am rigorously excluded from and know absolutely nothing about. Even her arrival was a mystery. I arrived home from shopping one sunny spring morning to see what I thought was a piece of dirty white paper thrown down at the drive gate. When I got out of the car to collect the mall, I walked across to remove the eyesore. It was only then that I realised that the dirty white paper was in actual fact a dirty, and sick, white cat. I picked her up and put her in the back of the car and was rewarded with a creaky purr.

There was something about her, perhaps the arrogant set of her little Roman nose, that reminded me of Tiny, most beloved of all my cats' company, plus the fact that Tiny had also been white and, like this cat, very sick when she first came into my life.

As I lifted her out of the car John, my husband, came over from the vegetable patch. 'What ever is that?' he asked. 'A white cat - someone has thrown her down at our gate.' I ignored the disparaging note in his voice. 'It's Tiny back!' I added.

Knowing my firm belief in reincarnation he knew what I meant - Tiny had been dead for some fifteen years, but he ignored the suggestion. 'She doesn't look white to me!' was all he said.

When the vet saw her he said she had a cat flu and was also in kitten. He pronounced a fifty-fifty chance of recovery, adding that if we were able to improve her condition quickly he could spay her before she had the kittens, which would be much better for her. Six months later when she came into full coat in the autumn she was a very beautiful cat who lived up to the name my daughter, in a moment of optimism, had given her when she first arrived: Sheba.

It soon became obvious that she had been a house pet. Not only did she calmly take it for granted that she would be a house cat, and moreover one whose right it was to commandeer the best chair, but she was also perfectly house-trained and very knowledgeable about such things as fridges and their contents, and can openers and how they were used to open cans of cat food.

She seemed such a helpless sort of pampered pet that we were beside ourselves with worry when she disappeared for twenty-four hours. However, she returned home none the worse. Five years later she still takes herself off on prolonged excursions.

The longest, to date, has been four days. She always sets off in the same direction, way across the paddock behind the house and heading for the creek that runs through the middle of the property. Occasionally we see her when we ourselves are riding or walking about the place, sunning herself on the creek bank; more often we do not catch so much as a glimpse of a whisker.

When we least expect her she will return, sitting on the kitchen window ledge demanding entry. Hers to command, ours to obey. When I see her sitting there I hurry to the door, too delighted to have her home even to mind that she rushes past me without so much as a 'prrt!' of thanks as I hold the door open for her. Sheba - beautiful, arrogant Sheba - is home again, safe and sound - that's all that matters!

To see her draped elegantly over a chair, a somnolent cloud of white fur, sometimes so fast asleep that she actually falls off, it seems impossible to imagine that she could possibly fend for herself for an hour, let alone four days and nights. Yet since her condition when she comes home is no worse than when she leaves, it is quite obvious that she is capable of doing so. How she does it, where she goes and what she does, is her secret - and hers alone.

It is possibly this ability of cats to lead two lives at once - their known, or family life and their secret, personal cat's life - that makes some people avow that they dislike cats. For many people, animals kept as pets should be there - twenty four hours a day - to be pets. But this is not the cat's way.

Much as she may love her home and her creature comforts, above all she treasures her precious independence. Part of this independence is the right to bestow her affections on whom she will - or not to bestow them at all! I sometimes think that if anyone is the pet in the relationship between cat and man, it is man!

The average well-adjusted cat who is in command of her life and the people in it has a lifestyle to be envied. She has a comfortable home with willing servants to obey her every whim - to open doors when required, serve meals at appointed times, to pamper and to cosset her and see she lacks for nothing. What does she do in return? Exactly as she pleases!

She does no work other than to catch the occasional marauding mouse, and that, after all, is really sport. She refuses to be trained to do anything useful on command like the dog or the horse. If it so pleases her she stays out all night about her own mysterious business, calmly ignoring all commands, entreaties and blandishments to return to hearth and home. In some curious way, by her very disdain and aloofness she makes us pathetically grateful when she does condescend to bestow a caress or purr upon us. Truly we are at worst her slaves, at best her pets. She is a goddess indeed holding over us the final threat - she will walk out and go and live elsewhere if she finds a place more to her liking.

It is her air of mystery that keeps us in thrall; and just a little afraid of her. The gentlest fireside tabby can become a tiger when the moon is full and she stalks her prey.

Have you ever come across your cat when she is intent upon a mouse hole? If you are noticed at all, it will be with a chilling glare that says more plainly than any spoken language could that your presence is most unwelcome. You are clumsy, noisy and above all interfering. Kindly remove your intrusive presence with all speed and without delay! Yet an hour or so later that same cat will stalk into the kitchen and coolly demand instant service. The hunt was unsuccessful and she is hungry. Or it was successful, and now she needs milk to wash it down. And it was rather chilly by that mouse hole so will you please switch on the electric radiator or stoke up the fire so that she can settle down for a good wash in comfort!

Sometimes however, even in the best-regulated cat lives catastrophe can occur and Puss may find herself homeless and totally without human friends. What happens then? Providing she is in possession of her health and faculties it is quite amazing how even the most pampered pussies can 'flip', as it were, to the reverse side of their dual nature and become a self- sufficient hunter and predator. The average dog, from the moment he leaves the security of mother and nest, is looking for one thing - a friend he can revere and look up to, a leader he can follow through life. Not so the cat. She simply does not need people in the same way; she can be physically and emotionally independent, if necessary.

It is because, like us, she knows that we either adore cats or we hate them. We admire or we fear them,

The poet Oliver Hereford, in just four short lines, very neatly phrased both the essential difference between dogs and cats and what makes us in thrall to cats - they flatter us!

> *To someone very good and just,*
> *Who has proved worthy of her trust,*
> *A cat will sometimes condescend -*
> *The dog is everybody's friend.*

There is an old proverb that says, 'God gave man the cat in order that he might have the pleasure of caressing the tiger'. It is probably the 'jungle beast' side of cats as much as the domestic pet that draws us to them. We are fascinated that such divergent dual personalities should exist in so small a frame. It is this facet of cats that has drawn poets, writers and artists to her down the centuries and inspired people like Carl Van Vechten to write whole books on the subject. His book dealing with the curious character of cats was first published in America in 1920 and is aptly called *The Tiger in the House.*

It is only when we come to terms with this side of the cat and can respect the wild animal that is part of even the most cossetted domestic pet that we will have a worthwhile relationship with 'the lion on the mat'.

Chapter 2
The Chooser and the Chosen

If anyone would doubt the true status of the cat as a goddess in today's world they should pause and reflect. Many cat lovers, perhaps most, will confess quite blatantly that they 'adore' cats.

I know I have certainly said that myself many times. The meaning of 'adore', according to the Oxford dictionary, is *to regard with deep respect and affection, worship as divine, offer reverence to.*

According to that definition, those of us who adore cats are certainly acknowledging her ancient status of goddess!

An animal rights group in Britain has a meditation movement: all who care for animals are asked to join in meditation for them at 9 p.m. each evening, wherever they maybe. One of the suggested prayers is the following invocation to Bast, the great cat goddess.

> *Bast, great goddess of cats, the golden Bast, I seek your protection for [here name any particular animal in need of special care] and your energy and intelligence to combat the cruel abusers of animals in this world and to allow animals to escape the enslavement of those who wish them harm.*

The cat may still have a long way to go to reach the status she once held in Ancient Egypt, but I do feel that people are becoming more 'cat conscious'. I have been struck recently by the number of people, particularly men, who have confessed to me their liking, often bordering on devotion, for cats. Usually they add that this is a new dimension in their lives, and that hitherto they had always been 'dog people'.

Perhaps it is no coincidence that the rise in the cat's status coincides with the feminist movement. Cats, whatever their actual sex, are always thought of as representing the feminine principles in life. The feminist movement, in its struggle to liberate women, has probably done as much or more for men by freeing them to admit and express the feminine side of their nature. For a man to confess a liking for cats is no longer considered odd, and neither is the cat peculiarly linked with spinsters (a connection that no doubt harks back to the Middle Ages, the dark ages indeed for Puss, when cats were burned to death with witches and the only real sanctuary for them was in convents). I think most people today would agree with Janet Lloyd, who wrote:

> *I find it most peculiar that*
> *They mock the spinster with her cat,*
> *But beam through sentimental fog*
> *Each time the bachelor walks his dog.*

Cats of course are neither sexist nor racist; but choose their people for sublimer reasons, and probably show better judgement than we do when we choose cats! For indeed people who live with cats (I won't call them cat owners, for who would have the temerity to dare to own a goddess?) can be roughly divided into the choosers and the chosen, with a few overlapping categories in between. There are those who buy cats and those who have cats thrust upon them, those who just acquire cats and those who are acquired by cats. The choosers and the chosen. Most cat devotees fall into one or both of these categories during their lives. When I look back over my years with cats I often remember them in this way - like dear old Muggins, who chose me way back when I was still in my teens.

It was one of those sultry summer afternoons that are typical of the English summer - after three hot days a thunderstorm comes. It was a Sunday, and after a somewhat desultory game of tennis we were recuperating limply in deck chairs with tall glasses of my mother's special home-made lemonade.

My father broke the silence. 'Wherever has that cat come from?' he asked.

Following his gaze I saw an incredibly plain and immensely pregnant black-and-white cat waddling purposefully towards us.

As my eye fell on her, up went her tail in greeting. Her mouth opened in a pink mew as she shouted to me for all the world as if we were old friends. Without so much as a glance at any other member of the family she trotted purposefully over to me, rubbed her head against my outstretched hand and began to purr.

'You are an ugly old muggins!' I told her. But the tone of my voice must have cancelled out the lack of courtesy in my greeting, for she only purred louder. From that moment on she was my cat, or I was her person - I never did work out quite which! She had also acquired a name, Mrs Muggins, more often affectionately known as 'Old Mug'.

Then there was Tiny, dear diminutive Tiny, so terribly frail in body, so immensely strong in character, whom I bought sight unseen as a three-week-old kitten from a Scottish breeder. She was dispatched in a cardboard box on the overnight express from Aberdeen to London at three months old - the most pathetic, undernourished, parasite-ridden scrap of hair and bones I have ever seen. Precious, priceless Tiny, who was my closest companion for ten years.

Closer in time there was Honey, the Abyssinian - aristocratic, arrogant and wildly extrovert - whom I purchased as a kitten;

Tilly, daughter of a famed ratter, a mongrel moggy almost as plain as Muggins and very like her in so many ways, who travelled from England to Tasmania and across the sea again to Victoria; Samantha, the half-dead kitten who somehow escaped the eye and bullet of the previous owner of a property we purchased.

When we moved in the wife told us that her husband had shot all the kittens so that they wouldn't be a nuisance to us. But he hadn't shot Samantha; she was often a nuisance to us but we loved her dearly and eventually took her with us to another property.

Nearer still in time there is Sheba, thrown away like so much garbage at my gate; Tabitha the terrible, whose mother is half Siamese and half Burmese, who was selected as a kitten from a neighbour's litter; Kit, as diminutive and frail as Tiny, bought in a pet shop by my daughter for $2.50.

Whatever made you buy a cat?' I asked. We already had five cats in the family.

'She looked at me and said, "Buy me" ', was the prompt reply from my passionately cat-loving seventeen-year-old daughter. Adding, with a logic that brooked no argument, 'You write about talking with animals. Well, she talked to me. She said "Buy me!" and I did.'

Kit was in almost as bad a physical state as Tiny was when I bought her, and had as many brushes with death before she reached maturity. Perhaps she did see in Ruth the needed saviour and it was in fact she and not my daughter who actually did the choosing.

Witches and cats go together like bread and cheese. Mrs Walters was the local witch in the tiny English hamlet in the heart of rural Staffordshire where I was born and spent all my early years. She was one of the smallest people (physically) I

14

Kit

have ever known, and she kept the only store in the village, a tiny shop selling bread, biscuits, sweets and basic provisions operating from the scullery at the back of her cottage.

However bright the sun on the little green at the front of the cottage it never seemed to penetrate to the back, and a chill always struck me as I moved into the shadow between the dark privet hedges that bordered the pathway; and no matter how warm the day I would often shiver as I turned the corner and stood in the dank shade of the old yew tree that kept the whole of her back yard in shadow.

It added a thrill of excitement to shopping at Mrs Walters' that was quite missing in any other shop. She herself did not frighten me. In fact I liked the old lady, feeling something of the affinity that so often exists between the very young and the very old. Just occasionally I was sent by my mother, but more often my visits were more illicit: I went to buy a pennyworth of sweets or a halfpenny stick of chocolate, or, if I was very rich, one of those delicious bags of sherbet with a long stick of black liquorice stuck in it.

Best of all I liked it when she had to weigh my purchase: there was something about the diminutive little old lady with her grey hair neatly scraped up into a bun on top of her head, standing on the wooden box she kept for the purpose and peering at her old-fashioned brass scales through a gigantic magnifying glass, that delighted me.

More than anything else though I liked her cats. Perhaps it was our mutual admiration for these creatures that shrank the years between us. She always had a large family of cats, smooth ones, fluffy ones, big ones, little ones - they were all loved and well cared for and most of them had just walked in.

My father had told me that cats put a secret sign outside true cat lovers' houses to let other cats know that here was a 'soft touch' where they could be sure of a welcome, a fire to sit by and a saucer of milk. Gypsies, he told me, did the same thing: they too left secret signs outside the homes of people who would treat them well and those who would not.

At that time I was a frustrated cat owner. Like most farms we had our complement of cats, three-parts wild, half-starved creatures who only put in an appearance round the cow sheds at milking time for the twice daily ration of milk which supplemented their diet of rats and mice. But in spite of all efforts to befriend them they remained obstinately wild. We had pet cats from time to time, but they always met with disaster. Smut was run over by the milk truck early one morning. Her kitten was killed in the machinery that pumped up water for the house and ran the milking machine. Fluff, the beautiful grey Persian given to me by a distant cousin from a neighbouring farm, met his end because of his total inability to learn house manners, and Ginger, the ginger tom kitten captured after a day-long hunt in the barns and hay-sheds of another farm, took one horrified look at our kitchen and shot under the dresser from where he howled and spat all the feline abuse and swearwords he could muster at our maid, spruce and clean in starched cap and apron. With one eye on the door he waited his chance and when it came, fled for the barns, his natural habitat, and joined our band of farm cats.

So, with my love for cats seeming to be forever thwarted, it was no small wonder that Mrs Walters large and happy cat family should be such a draw. While I made my small purchase or spun out the time by chatting to the old lady there would always be one furry body rubbing against my small bare legs, at least one voice throbbing with pleasure under my childish caresses. Undisputed leader of this cat family was Trix. A huge fluffy black tom, he was at least twice the size of Mickey, our diminutive Yorkshire terrier-cross dog with whom he had a long-standing feud.

If ever Mickey came to the shop with me I had to be sure either to pick him up or put him on a lead when I got there, for he had a fighting spirit quite out of proportion to his stature and was prepared to do battle with Trix whenever and wherever he met him - even though he was quite amicably inclined towards all other cats. The hostility was mutual, and on more than one occasion we had rushed out of the house to bring Mickey indoors when we observed Trix surveying the world from our garden wall, at least a quarter of a mile from his own home.

Perhaps my father was right about the secret sign; certainly no one else in the village ever seemed to get stray cats while Mrs Walters lived. It was shortly after her death at the advanced age of ninety-seven that Muggins trotted across the lawn that sultry summer afternoon to become the first cat that I could truly say was mine, not because I bought her or even chose her, but because she chose me. She was the first but by no means the last stray to come and live with us. When Mrs Walters died I think the secret sign must have been put up at our gate.

These cats who walk in do not always only satisfy their own need. So often they fill an empty place in someone's heart as well as in their home and give much more than they receive. Sometimes they almost seem to come for a purpose.

'Why' was one such, and by his action he perhaps answered the question that was his name. Here is his story as told to me by his loving and grateful mistress.

He came without introduction or reason and stayed. He was a smallish cat, about a year old, and his charcoal fur shone with wellbeing and there was spring in all his movements. We called him 'Why'.

Soon after he moved in he appointed himself official escort to all family members walking to the bus that ran at the end of the street. He would bounce ahead and lead the way for the two block walk, detouring over a garden wall if a dog appeared, but always reappearing further along the street to continue his escort right to the bus stop. He waited till the bus came, then darted off homeward at great speed.

One Saturday morning, with only an hour before the shops closed, I remembered a birthday present I had to buy and headed for the bus. As usual, Why was well ahead of me as I hurried down the street. Suddenly, about halfway there, he seemed to falter, gave a slight roll, and collapsed quite limp on the footpath. I ran to him and stooped to pick him up. His eyes were wide open. I checked and he was still breathing, but his little body felt like jelly.

My hitherto urgent errand quite forgotten, I picked him up and hurried home. What to do? Though the vet had Saturday morning surgery he was two suburbs away and I had no car. I laid him gently on a towel on the kitchen floor beneath the watchful eye of my son and went to seek help from my neighbours. They were out - on both sides. I ran back inside to find my son calmly munching on a Vegemite sandwich and no sign of Why.

'He's OK, Mum', he told me. 'He just got up and skipped out the back door.'

I reached the back steps in time to see him jump onto the fence which he trotted along in perfect balance before leaping another metre or so onto the shed roof, where he settled down to a good wash in the warm sun. I was still puzzled over his 'fit' when I went back indoors and met my husband coming in the side door from the garage.

'The bus has had an accident!' he told me. 'I've just been helping to get the people out! It hit a truck - no one was killed but there was blood and glass everywhere. Two people looked pretty badly injured. Some doctors and a nurse came and the ambulances are on the way.'

'I should have been on that bus!' I gasped. 'Only Why had a fit - or ... something.' I tailed off, then as the implication of Why's fit struck me - 'Oh, my God! That cat could have saved my life!'

When I had explained what had happened to my husband I went and found Why. He had exchanged his high perch for a shady spot on the lawn. I rubbed his tummy in gratitude and said, 'Maybe we shouldn't call you 'Why' any longer!'

My own early attempts to choose a cat having ended in disaster, it was not until I went to boarding school at the tender age of seven that I had a chance to really get to know cats and learn first-hand just how well a cat can choose - and having chosen, set about organising things very much to her own advantage!

I was sent to a small private boarding school near Warwick in the heart of the English Midlands, run by two 'bachelor' ladies, Miss Williams and Miss Burton (known to the pupils as Will and Bert). They may have owned and run a school, but they themselves were owned and run by two cats, Toby and Whiskers. Toby belonged to Miss Williams, or she belonged to him, and Whiskers to Miss Burton. Toby was a middle-aged coal-black shorthair who was getting rather hard of hearing and sedate. Whiskers was strikingly handsome, much more debonair and dashing, a Silver Tabby shorthair. Both cats had just walked into the school and established themselves.

There were only about 120 girls in the school altogether and of these only about twenty were boarders. A mere handful, about eight at the most, were full-time boarders, so that at weekends at any rate it was more like living in a large family, albeit all female, than a boarding school. During the week there would be two tables in the dining room: a long trestle table for the juniors and a smaller heavy oak dining table presided over by the joint head- mistresses, one at each end, and occupied by the resident staff and the senior girls. At weekends when our numbers were depleted we all sat at this table.

This was Whiskers' and Toby's table too. At breakfast time a large pile of bowls would be brought in and placed in front of Miss Burton. At the top were two smaller bowls. These she filled first, in the winter, with porridge, in the summer, with cornflakes and solemnly passed them down the table to Miss Williams, who added sugar and milk, put one down for Toby who was sitting by her chair with his own place mat, and passed the other back to Miss Burton who placed it in front of Whiskers.

At lunchtime the whole procedure was repeated, only this time it was Miss Williams, who always carved the meat, who had the pile of plates in front of her. A slice of meat was placed in each dish. They were then passed up to Miss Burton who added a small helping of vegetables and gravy; passed Whiskers' plate down to him and sent Toby's back up the table to Miss Williams.

After the cats, any teachers at the table were served. Then the prefects, and so down the scale. The curious thing was that I never remember hearing anyone voice any resentment over the priority given to the cats. They were in fact adored by all the girls, who seemed to think it only right and proper that they should be treated with such respect. Without exception we all knew that the quickest way to favour was to be seen to be a cat worshipper, and I am equally sure that the quickest way to get expelled would have been to have treated either cat with cruelty or even disrespect!

When anyone had a birthday it was the custom to take Miss Williams and Miss Burton a piece of birthday cake in their holy of holies, the elegant drawing room where they themselves took afternoon tea. The cosy scene of the two genteel 'maiden ladies' on either side of a blazing log fire, with the tea trolley between them, and a cat and a saucer (on its place mat of course) by the side of each, is firmly entrenched in my memory. Those two cats certainly knew what they were doing when they chose to live in a girls' boarding school!

I spent five years at this school, and by the time I left Toby was a very deaf, but very venerable old gentleman and the dashing Whiskers was middle-aged, though still the most handsome cat I had ever seen. As for me, I was a confirmed cat worshipper with a deeply ingrained belief that while all animals are equal, cats are a lot more equal than others!

One of my 'special' chosen cats was Tilly. In the early years of my marriage we were living on a large Bedfordshire farm that specialised in grain growing, where a good staff of farm cats was a necessity. We were getting a little low in numbers, and a friend of mine who kept a grocer's shop had a female cat who was a superb ratter. She promised me first choice of the kittens from the forthcoming litter.

There were three kittens, and when they were only a few days old I went to choose mine. Two were handsome tabby-and-white males, very like their mum, and the third was a black-and-white female. Nan was most surprised when I told her which one I wanted. 'I didn't think anyone would want her!', she exclaimed. 'A female - and so plain!'

Well, I do!' I said. 'I like her.' Nan made no more demur, obviously pleased that her ugly duckling was bespoken.

I hadn't had a black-and-white cat since dear old Muggins all those years ago. Was that why I chose this one, so very like that other dear feline friend, or was it, as I told myself, because I secretly agreed with Nan and thought that if I didn't have her no one would? When she came to live with us at eight weeks old, Tilly made it quite plain that though she may have been born a warehouse cat, she was not going to grow up a granary cat. As often as I returned her there she made the journey back. It was obvious that her determination and perseverance was far greater than mine, and so I conceded victory to Tilly.

Her cool appraisal of the situation and her calm decision to move up the social ladder and become a house cat won my admiration and respect; her delightful personality soon won my love as well - so much so that when we left England to live in Australia a couple of years later I found homes for all the other cats, including Honey, my beautiful pure-bred Abyssinian, but took Tilly with me. But near tragedy was to strike before that day.

I was sitting out in the sun in the front garden shelling peas for Sunday lunch when my neighbour turned into the drive.

'I'm terribly sorry;' she told me as she pulled the car up, 'but I am afraid I've run over one of your cats.'

'Which one?' I asked tersely.

'Oh, not your Abyssinian, a black-and-white one. It was when I was going into church. I was late, and she was dead anyway, so I thought I'd tell you on the way back.'

I pushed the peas to one side, bade her an even terser farewell, and went to find John, who was digging in the vegetable garden at the back of the house. He looked down at the spade in his hand. 'I'll get her straight away and bury her.' He set off towards the road on his sad mission with five-year-old Graham trotting beside him to 'help'.

A couple of minutes later Graham was running back yelling, 'Mummy! Mummy! She's not dead!'

He was followed more slowly by John, holding the spade before him on which he had gently laid the inert form of my dear Tilly. I ran to meet them. They were right; she was not dead - not quite.

I remembered the time six months previously when we had been interrupted at breakfast by a knock on the kitchen door.

John had opened it to a young couple, the girl in tears and the young man holding before him on outstretched hands (much as John now had her on the spade) a 'dead' Tilly.

'I'm very sorry;' he had said, 'But I am afraid your cat was hit by a car in front of us.'

John had reached to take her and as he did so, she had sprung to life and vanished at high speed somewhere in the garden. When I had eventually found her, the only injury I could see was a slightly scratched ear.

But this time there was no springing to life; her 'death' looked very much for real. Carefully we laid her in the back of the station wagon, as this seemed the safest, flattest, quietest place; above all, it was out of the reach of inquisitive dogs and children.

Then I hurried indoors to phone the vet at his home, only to be told he was out on a~call. I rang that number to find he had left for another call, happily only a mile or so away from us. I tracked him down at that number and he promised to come straight away.

After he had examined her carefully he straightened up. 'Well...', he replied slowly and carefully to my - anxious, 'will she live?' 'Well... if she were a dog or a human she would almost certainly be dead now, but as she is a cat I think she has about a fifty-fifty chance.

She had head injuries and a badly damaged hip and was in severe shock, which hadn't been helped by the hour-and-a-half she had lain in the dust at the side of the road in the hot summer sun.

I asked him if he intended to take her back with him to his little animal hospital but he told me that, providing I could find a way to more or less immobilise her, he would rather not, because she might just give up and die if she found herself in strange surroundings when she regained consciousness.

I felt sure he was right. I borrowed a dog-carrying crate from a friend who bred miniature Dachshunds and laid her carefully in it. This I carried into the house and put in the spare bedroom and devoted every minute I could spare to nursing her - mostly just being with her, persuading her that I cared, making sure that she didn't give in. She aborted the kittens she was carrying, but by the time the sailing date arrived (she was going on ahead of us because of the time she would have to spend in quarantine on arrival) she was fully recovered, apart from the limp that the vet assured me would be with her always. It wasn't. The enforced rest of a month at sea and two months in quarantine worked wonders. when we met again in Tasmania, three months after she left England, she was 100 per cent sound and fit.

That was a day I shall never forget. Although it was midsummer in the southern hemisphere the rain was coming down in ultra-soaking sheets, true Tasmanian style. Tilly and Peggy; the dog we had also brought out from England, had been sent over from Melbourne on the Princess of Tasmania and we were to meet them at the docks at Devonport. We were told to go aboard and collect them ourselves from the kennels right at the top of the little ship. Up there, with the rain coming down in a grey wall, I could see no kennels.

'Where are they?' I asked. But before John could answer I heard a joyous yowl.

'Tilly!' I shouted, and was answered by another. It was then I saw the row of little boxes that were built into the top deck. I pounced on the one with the miaow in it while John located Peggy. I unbolted the door and with another yowl and a 'prrt!' of joy, Tilly was in my arms.

She stayed there for the twenty-five-mile ride to our new home, looking at the strange scenery with the greatest of interest and punctuating her ecstatic Te Deum with little 'yowl!'s and 'prrt!'s of affection.

Tilly was one of the few cats, other than my pedigree breeding cats, that I never had spayed. I don't quite know why. I always kept one or two kittens from a litter and managed to find good homes for them. Fortunately she was not a very prolific cat, never having more than two litters a year and sometimes only two kittens at a time.

Our Tasmanian farm was up its own winding, hilly lane more than half a mile off the road. Here she was safe at least from speeding motorists but not, alas, from other perils. One day she limped Into the kitchen with a grotesquely swollen front paw, howling in agony. A great rabbiter, she had fallen victim to one of those barbarously cruel inventions of man, the steel-jawed trap. Fortunately whoever had set it had also released her.

Four years after settling in Tasmania we moved again, this time over to the mainland of Australia - Victoria. Our move this time seemed an even more gigantic undertaking than the one from England, for in addition to ourselves and household furniture we had a semi-trailer load of animals, including of course Tilly with two of her daughters and one of her sons. They would be making the Bass Strait crossing in the travelling pen in which Tilly herself had come out from England.

Everybody was loaded, including Betsy, the pet sheep, the dog, Tilly's three children, the house cow, the calves she was rearing, and all the donkeys and their foals; everyone but Tilly. I called - I searched - I hunted and I called again. There was no Tilly. Finally the truck had to leave for the docks at Burnie.

I did the round of the neighbours and asked them to look after her if she turned up and let me know; somehow I would make arrangements to get her over to Victoria. Sadly I took one last look around the empty house, gave one last call in the garden and climbed into the car belonging to friends who were taking the children and me to the plane at Devonport. John, who was taking our own car by sea with the animals, had already left.

As Bruce switched on the ignition, I took one last look round and there, unbelievably, trotting towards us across the yard, was Tilly!

'Stop!' I shouted, and before he had switched off I was out of the car and had swept up my little friend into my arms. Bruce must have broken all speed records as he raced to Burnie - the opposite direction from the airport. We got to the docks in time to bundle Tilly into the travelling crate with her son and daughters, and to Devonport in time to catch the plane. Twenty-four hours later we were once more all reunited in a new home.

Poor Tiny. Her passion for rabbiting, which had already given her so many near squeaks, was to be her undoing. Eighteen months later, on the twins' eighth birthday (she herself was a week older than them), she crawled into the kitchen in a state of great distress. Within half an hour she was dead, victim of 10:80 rabbit poison - another of man's less pleasant inventions.

Dear Tiny, so loved and so lovable and so like that other dear plain black-and-white cat, Muggins, who so many years ago had chosen me. Could it be that in choosing Tiny, I had recognised my old friend back again and merely returned the compliment - as she had once chosen me, I now chose her? It is a thought, anyway, and one which brings to mind Sheba - a cat who shares my present life.

Perhaps it was not mere accident that caused her to be thrown away, like so much rubbish, at my drive gate. Perhaps when I said to John, 'I've been given Tiny back again!' I was speaking no less than the literal truth. This time I had been chosen as all those years ago I chose.

There are so many similarities between the Sheba of today and the Tiny of yesterday, the white coat being only one. True, Sheba's coat is long and flowing whereas Tiny's was short, and both her eyes are melon-coloured, whereas only one of Tiny's was - the other being a brilliant sapphire blue. Sheba's body is somewhat stronger and more robust than that of poor little Tiny, but like her she suffers from intermittent bouts of eczema if I do not watch her diet; again like Tiny, her bad start in life has resulted in a premature loss of many of her teeth and she too has a leonine profile with a chin so strong it Is seldom seen on any cat but the 'king of the beasts' himself.

She learned Tiny's favourite party trick - jumping through the hoop made by a person's clasped hands and outstretched arms - so quickly one would suspect she had learned it before. Like Tiny she has a passion for yeast tablets and again like her she will hook them daintily out of the jar with a paw, usually her left one.

When I wake in the morning and see Sheba's face so close to my own (she sleeps on a beanbag close to the top of my bed) or reach out a hand sleepily in the night just to check she is there and feel the vibration and hear the rumble of her purr (sometimes she imprisons my hand with gently extended claws in order to give it a few vigorous licks of affection), I can be forgiven for thinking that my old friend has returned to share another incarnation with me.

The Chooser and the Chosen; which is which? And does it matter so long as the end result - the getting together - is achieved? Sometimes the manner of the choosing can have an element of the mystical. Derek Tangye writes about just such a choice in his delightful book Lama.

In spite of the fact that he had been brought up in an entirely 'dog household' arid had convinced himself that he not only hated cats but was actually allergic to them, one cat eventually won him over: Monty, the magnificent marmalade-and-white cat that shared his and his wife Jeannie's life for some sixteen years.

When Monty died Derek refused to have another cat. It was Monty he had loved; he had not been converted to loving all cats - or so he reasoned. To his wife's entreaties he returned only an adamant 'No'. But on the evening that Monty died Derek had said, impulsively, from his deep subconscious, without - as he said - a trace of reason.

'On one condition only will I ever have a cat again; and that is if a black cat comes to the cottage in a storm - and we never can find where it comes from.'

On Easter Sunday, almost a year after Monty's death - a year in which well-meaning friends had tried to give them a kitten, a year in which Jeannie had wanted a kitten and Derek had resisted - a tremendous gale blew up from the south. The rain and the wind roared in from the sea so that the Tangyes, in their Cornish cottage, had to raise their voices to hear each other speak.

In a pause in their conversation and a slight lull in the storm Derek heard a different sound. It was a miaow. He opened the door, letting, as he says, part of the storm into the room - and with it a small, totally black cat.

Sometimes the choosing that takes place between cat and person, person and cat, is so decisive that I cannot help but think there must be something more than mere chemical attraction between the two. Many years ago I had a litter of identical Brown Tabby shorthair kittens. They were like four little bumblebees, every stripe and swirl on their rich sable coats matched. Only their personalities were different.

One of them was so inordinately shy that whenever anyone, even a member of the family, came into the room he would dive beneath the nearest piece of furniture and only emerge if the feet he saw were familiar.

One afternoon a charming middle-aged couple came to collect one of the kittens, a female they had ordered over the phone. To my utter amazement the shy one came out from his hidey-hole and sat actually on the toe of the man's shoe, gazing up into his face with that single-minded round stare that only a cat, a kitten at best, can muster. I could hardly believe it.

The Brown Tabby Kittens

He sat there, and he went on sitting there. His sister was already happily purring in the wife's arms, chooser and chosen mutually satisfied, and the other two kittens of the litter were playing about the room. Still he went on sitting, his unwavering gaze fixed on the man's face. After some discussion between husband and wife, during which the kitten never moved, they decided to take him as well. When the man bent to pick him up I still expected him to make a bolt for it, but no, with a contented purr he settled into his hand and looked across at his sister as if to say, 'I'm coming too' and at me as if to say goodbye; then, purring triumphantly, he returned his gaze to the man's face.

From time to time over the years I heard news of him, and always I was told of his extraordinary and exceptional devotion to the husband, a devotion which was fully reciprocated.

This was one of the most blatant examples of choosing on the part of a cat I have ever witnessed. I often wonder what sparked it off - recognition perhaps?

Chapter 3
Aristo-cat and Alleycat Moggies All!

'The colonel's lady and Judy O'Grady are sisters under the skin.' So the saying goes. I strongly suspect that exactly the same applies to pussies as to people! Whatever shade the fur, turn it back and you will just find a moggy wearing it.

This is not to say that all cats are the same - far from it; the one characteristic that all cats share is their difference. Their fierce determination to be a one-off, an individual. Being a pedigree puss with a lineage as long as your arm may give a cat a perfect excuse to behave like the superior being she is convinced she is; but it does not mean that the alley cat, or 'ordinary' mongrel moggy won't have as much, or more, sheer arrogance and disdain.

It is possibly precisely because the cat is so sure of her own superiority, so much her own person, that we who love cats often do so with a devotion that really does border on worship. We accept her valuation of herself.

The cats who have kept me company through life have been about equally divided into alley cats and aristo cats. Curiously enough it was plain old Muggins, with no possible hint of aristocratic lineage, who was to be the launching pad for my flight into the amazing world of pedigree cats. She was an old cat when the startlingly handsome white tom cat with blazing amber eyes appeared in our little village. Vigorous and virile, he came from no one knew where, stayed about ten days, during which he took his pick of the local females and vanquished ignominiously the local males, and then vanished as mysteriously as he had come.

The litter that Muggins produced a couple of months later consisted of only two kittens - a 'pigeon pair'. The male was black and white, a replica of the old lady herself, while the other kitten, a female, was white. Pure white, except for two sooty smudges on the top of her round little billiard ball of a head. In years to come I was to look anxiously on my white kittens for these marks which in Gussie, the first of many, I deemed to be blemishes.

I called her Gussie after 'Gorgeous Gussie' Moran who, the year before (this was the spring of 1950) had hit the headlines and captured the imagination of the public with her sensational win at Wimbledon and her equally sensational tennis wear.

Gussie was indeed gorgeous, in my eyes at least. I had never seen a very new White kitten before and I was quite entranced. The tiny pink paws were so like hands and the little round face with closed eyes and pink nose and lips was that of a tiny flying doll.

In spite of the fact that Muggins' fecundity had made me vow never to keep a female kitten unless I had a home waiting for it (1 had a good home lined up for the tom) and the old superstition that white cats are as unlucky as black cats are purported to be lucky ('Kiss the black cat and grow fat - kiss the white cat and grow lean,' goes the old proverb), nothing on earth would have induced me to consign my precious white kitten to oblivion - or even place her in another home. From the moment she was born she was 'my' cat in a way no other cat had ever been.

Far from being unlucky, she was the luckiest cat I have ever had, both for me and for herself. She lived to the ripe old age of seventeen and for all that time she was dearly loved. She introduced me to the fascinating world of pedigree cats, and it was through her that I bought Tiny, most precious and greatly loved of all my cats' company.

Gussie

Gussie and her brother were the last kittens old Muggins ever had, but not the last of the line, for Gussie was to have many kittens before she was eventually spayed at seven years old. Whatever the colour of the sire, Gussie always had a percentage of white kittens, usually about half the litter. This I thought was marvellous. In those days my ignorance of catty matters was so profound that I didn't even know that in cats white is a dominant colour, which means that a white cat will always have some white kittens, and that every white cat must have at least one white parent. It seemed that, superstition or not, people liked white cats. My kittens were always in demand - so much so that I even had people offering to pay for them!

Then one day I idly picked up a magazine in the newsagent's and discovered there was something called 'The Cat Fancy' - that cats were shown, and bred, and had pedigrees and price tags. I bought the magazine, found the address of this Cat Fancy and wrote to the Secretary of the Governing Council. It was a momentous letter. I discovered that there was a thing called a Supplementary Register and that any cat who conformed to the standard laid down for that particular variety could be registered in this, and that gradually by a grading-up process the descendants could become pedigree cats.

There was a breed known as British Shorthairs, and one of the recognised colours was white. Gussie it seemed did conform and was soon a registered cat!

As the owner of a registered cat I was launched into the world of pedigrees, breeding and showing. Cat people, I found, were a very friendly bunch. What is more, they were generous in sharing their knowledge, often gained by years of experience, with a rank newcomer like myself. The foremost authority and well-known judge of British Shorthairs, the author of a little book on the breed and breeder himself of some very fine British Blue cats, was the Rev. Basil Rees. He said that if I would contact him after he had finished judging at a forthcoming London show he would take me round afterwards and explain the placings to me.

Who could refuse such an offer? I went to my first ever cat show and duly made myself known to him. True to his word, he gave me well over an hour of his time. As he pointed out the good and bad points of the cats, and why he had placed them as he had, I realised that there was a great deal more to this cat breeding business than met the eye!

This, my first show, mesmerised me. Never in my wildest dreams had I imagined that cats could be so beautiful and so diverse. The Siamese, by far the largest group numerically, with their bat-like ears, their svelte coats and the gamin grace of their spidery limbs, amazed me with the incredible startling sapphire blue of their eyes. Almost equally startling were the blazing flame-coloured eyes of the Blue Persians staring haughtily at the gaping crowds. I was spellbound by the breathtaking beauty of the Chinchillas with their sparkling frosty coats and dramatically 'mascara'd' lids highlighting their round aquamarine eyes.

There were tabbies there with markings so clear, so symmetrical, they must surely have been painted by a master. And I had always thought tabbies 'ordinary'! But entranced though I was by the glamour and variety of the aristocats of the feline world, it was to the white cats that I kept returning. Particularly the shorthaired ones. I knew I was thoroughly biased, but all the same I was sure that Gussie could have held her own even in this company. Her father, I was sure, with his amazing amber eyes would have swept the board. Gussie's eyes were, alas, the lemon shade of her mothers'.

The cats that really took my fancy were the blue- eyed whites. The bright forget-me-not blue of their eyes was quite different to the deep sapphire of the Siamese, and combined with a coat as white as the newest snow and a shell-pink nose, lips and paw pads, they made a cat as ethereally beautiful as the fictional ice princess. I was determined to both own and breed these beautiful cats.

What I didn't know was that blue-eyed white cats are the most elusive to come by of all breeds, whether one is buying or breeding. Not only do the orange or yellow-eyed variety always far exceed in numbers the blue-eyed ones, but the dreaded deafness gene seems tied to the blue eyes. I have never heard of a deaf white cat with yellow or orange eyes; on the other hand, though all the deaf white cats seem to be blue-eyed, not all blue-eyed white cats are deaf. A blue-eyed white with perfect hearing is a prized and often priceless pussy.

But I knew none of all this then, and if I had it probably wouldn't have made any difference. I was enthralled by these beautiful cats and only knew I wanted one!

Finally, after months and months of searching and endless phone calls and letters, I located a breeder in Scotland who said she had a white female for sale. Both her parents and all four of her grandparents were blue-eyed whites. She was only just born and her eyes were not open yet, but she hoped they too would be blue. Without any hesitation I said I would have her.

A few weeks later the breeder wrote again to say that she was afraid that the kitten's eyes were not blue, but odd, (one blue and one yellow). However, she had a black smudge on her head which of course would fade, so she would not be deaf.

By now I had discovered that all white kittens, or nearly all, were born with sooty smudges - one, two, or three, just like fingerprints, on their heads. Talking to other breeders I had discovered that these smudges were not, as I had at first thought, unique to Gussie and her children, but that all white cats were born with them. However they always faded - sometimes in a few weeks, sometimes in a few months. This was the first time however that I heard it connected with deafness.

Odd eyes, I had discovered, did occur quite often in white cats. I wrote back and said I would still take the kitten. After all, one blue eye was better than none! As this was the only blue eye all my searching had unearthed it seemed I had better have her. Prophetic words: I have never had a cat with two blue eyes, or even another odd-eyed one!

By now, even though I was frustrated in my desire to breed blue-eyed cats, far from being put off the breed I was even more fascinated by the extraordinary challenge they presented and I resolved to find out more about them. I read everything I could find and talked at length to everyone I met who had anything to do with white cats. These people came up with the same information: only the blue-eyed ones were deaf, but not all blue- eyed ones, something under fifty per cent it would seem, and those that were deaf were invariably born pure white without the black smudges. Those 'blemishes', it seemed, were not blemishes at all but a sort of hallmark of soundness placed there by the celestial cat maker!

Genetically it would seem that blue-eyed whites are partial albinos. If they were pure albinos the eyes would be pink, not blue. The blue eyes incidentally glint red, not green, when caught in artificial light. It is often this red glow that is the first indication when the kitten opens its eyes that they will be the bright china blue of the white cat when they change from the dark cloudy blue that is the colour of every kitten's eyes when they first open.

This partial albinoism would appear to be linked with deafness, albeit not perfectly, or every blue-eyed white cat would be deaf. The dark smudges prevent the cat being even a partial albino and so break the link I could scarcely contain my impatience as I waited for 11 November, which was the day I was to collect my precious white kitten. That was the day of the big championship cat show in London and 'Whitehaugh Cream Cracker', the name on the pedigree already in my possession, was being sent down from Aberdeen on the night express along with her grandfather, 'Whitehaugh Frosty'. He was competing in the show and a London breeder had undertaken to exhibit him for his owner and despatch him back to Scotland afterwards. My kitten would be handed over to me at the show.

The moment I arrived at the hall I searched out Frosty's pen. It was well-covered in prize cards and among them the much-coveted Challenge Certificate; it was his third, so he was now entitled to be called Champion. It was well deserved. His coat was as sparkling as his name suggested, his eyes the deepest, brightest sky blue, and when I spoke to him he immediately responded. He was obviously not deaf.

I was still admiring him - the grandfather of my kitten - when the lady in charge of him returned to his pen. I made myself known. Where was my kitten?

I saw a shadow cross her face when she knew who I was; somehow it was as if a cold hand had touched me. Though I was anxious to hear what she had to say, my anxiety and disappointment was so strong that I hardly took in her words.

'My husband has gone home to fetch her,' she told me, looking up at the clock on the wall she added, 'He should be back in about twenty minutes or so.

I arranged to meet her back at Frosty's pen in half an hour. I spent the time walking around the hall and looking at the other cats. I saw them all in a haze. Somehow I was quite sure that something was wrong.

When we re-met and she handed me a small cardboard carton that felt far too light to contain a butterfly, let alone a cat, I knew I was right.

'I thought she was better at home,'she told me. 'She couldn't stay in this box all day, and besides - well, to tell the truth I was afraid to bring her this morning, you know, when the vets and that are here - bringing her in now, no one realises there is a cat in there.'

She looked at me, a wealth of meaning in her expression. I understood why she was reluctant to say more, for we were surrounded by people and cat shows are efficiently run affairs and very conscious of the health and wellbeing of the chief participants, the cats themselves. I thanked her for looking after her for me and bade her goodbye. As I turned to leave the hall she called after me. 'I do hope you can rear her!'

With these ominous words ringing in my ears I headed for the street and hailed a taxi. It was not the weight but the frailty of my burden that made me loath to take the bus or underground train. The box was so light and the inmate so still and so quiet that I wondered if I really had got a cat in there.

When I finally cut the string and opened the box three or four hours later in the kitchen at home, surrounded by my family, I was still tempted to wonder.

No-one spoke as I put my hand into the box and lifted out the smallest scrap of living cat I had ever seen.

'But - .... tiny!' breathed my sister. From then on it was inevitable that she should be 'Tiny - whatever the name on her pedigree.

'She's nothing but a scrap of bone and a hank of hair!' said my father.

'Good God!' was all my usually voluble mother could say. As for me - I was lost for words!

My father was right. There was no more to her than a hank of hair, strangely rough, coarse hair at that, and a scrap of bone. Bone that felt as light and fragile as that of a fledgling bird.

I turned her to face me, and in spite of everything I smiled. The only large thing about her were her eyes: one was the commonplace yellow that I was used to see looking at me from cats' faces, the other was the most brilliant sky-blue I had ever seen. The black smudge dabbed in a haphazard fashion over the yellow eye accentuated the oddity.

She stared straight back at me with those extraordinary eyes over the Roman nose that gave her face its air of arrogant aristocracy. She made it quite clear that she was not afraid, or that if she was, she certainly wasn't going to show it.

I held her level with my face and we took stock of each other; her gaze was unblinking, the tip of her tail twitched slightly and a small growl rumbled somewhere in her frame.

What spunk! I knew she was 'special' and that, come what may, I had to rear her.

Little did I know how hard it would be to keep that vow. Her microscopic stature was due to the fact that she was riddled with parasites, both worms internally and fleas externally. Once free of these she went down with enteritis and then with cat flu, after which she lost all her hair!

Three things kept her going: the coke-fired stove burning day and night in the living room where she lived for three months that cold English winter, my determination to rear her and, most important of all, her own enormous will to live.

When her hair fell out we dare not even let her move about the house from room to room What an extraordinary sight she presented, weighing just about one quarter of what a normal cat her age should weigh, skinny - and pink - and staring defiantly at the world with those amazing odd eyes.

It was Easter before she had sufficient coating of hair for me to dare let her out in the warm spring sun for a short while each day. For most of the past months her life had hung in the balance but in that time she had won the admiration, respect and love of the entire family and between her and myself a bond had been forged that nothing could sever.

I had learned an immense amount about cats, though I must admit that as far as character went Tiny was always such a determined individualist that more often than not she was the exception that proved the rule, rather than the rule itself!

I was of course even more determined to breed blue-eyed white cats. Tiny's remarkable character, plus her one brilliant blue eye, seemed to me only a shadow of what might be. I planned to send Gussie to be mated to a blue-eyed white stud cat.

Alas for planned parenthood! One night Gussie did not come in to bed and when she strolled in for breakfast in the morning with Tim, a handsome shorthaired brown tabby tom who was another member of our cat family, I knew by the look on their faces that I had been out-smarted. At least I knew something about the Cat Fancy now! I promptly registered Timmy in the Supplementary Register; with his beautiful plush black and sable coat without any trace of white markings he measured up well to the standard laid down for Shorthair Brown Tabbies.

I could always send Gussie away next time. (But there was to be no 'next time'. Gussie developed ovarian cysts and had to be spayed. The fates, it seemed, were not impressed with my ambition to breed white cats!)

When the kittens arrived, there were two white males, one of which died shortly after birth, and two brown tabbies, one male and one female.

Even my prejudiced eye could see that there was really nothing very special about the white kitten, whereas the brownies ... their heads were round as little apples, their short, plush coats a deep rich sable, and the clear black markings, identical on each, were like embossed velvet.

I duly registered all three kittens with my new prefix, 'Whiston'. I advertised the white at eight weeks and sold him as a pet - in fact I had such a response to my advertisement that I could have sold him at least seven times! - and entered my two little brownies for one of the big events in the cat calendar, the Kensington Kitten Show in London.

I was prompted to take this bold step by an article I had read about Brown Tabbies by one of the most prominent cat judges of the time. I wrote to her about my brownies and in fact through her I sold the male, but kept him on until after the show so that the two could go together. Their names were Tiger Tim and Tabitha Twitchet. I entered them in the catalogue as 'For Sale' but, by a happy chance, the printers missed this out. Tiger Tim of course was already sold and when I arrived back at the show hall after the judging and saw the awards on their pen I had no intention of selling Tabitha - far from it; I was going to breed Brown Tabbies.

I was absolutely amazed: both were placed well in every class they were entered in, winning awards as high as second even in very large classes of mixed breeds and competing against the progeny of illustrious champions. What is more, my 'ordinary' little tabbies were the centre of admiration from both breeders and general public.

If, as some people believe, people can come back after death as animals, then I am sure that Tabitha, in some former life, had been a star in the performing arts. I have never seen an animal before or since who so much enjoyed showing off and any form of publicity.

Whenever I hear anyone say that cat shows are cruel, I think of Tabitha, who loved them. When we were preparing for a show I never got out her travelling box until the last minute. If I did she would immediately get into it, ready to go - even leaving her food to do so! She would pose with such enthusiasm for photographers that when Monty, a well- known animal photographer, came to take photos of the cats he complained of Tabitha overposing!

'For Heavens sake!' he said in exasperation. 'Can't you stop that cat posing? I can't get a natural-looking shot of her!'

She was a glorious, happy, amusing extrovert. She loved travelling, she loved shows, she loved staying away from home whether we stayed in hotels or with friends. She was enormous fun to have around. The happy times we had together, coupled with her obvious enjoyment in a very successful show career, made up in large measure for my frustrations and disappointments with my white cats.

One eminent judge summed up her attitude to shows perfectly when she wrote of her in her judge's report: 'This cat is a real pleasure to judge. She obviously enjoys every minute of it and never stopped purring the whole time!'

She soon had an impressive pile of prize cards and by the time she was a young adult she was Champion Whiston Tabitha Twitchet. Her photo appeared in books and magazines not only in England, but in America as well. I found it hard to believe that my little star was the granddaughter of dear, plain old Muggins.

She was one of the few cats I have ever known who really seemed to enjoy being beautified. She didn't even mind being bathed. I found this out when she was about eight months old. The day before she was to go to a big London show she fell into a bucket of milk!

There was nothing for it but a bath. I used my own shampoo and dried her with the hair dryer. She made no objections and looked so beautiful afterwards that a bath before a show became routine. She loved being vacuum-cleaned with the upholstery attachment and would lie supine with half-closed eyes, her purring inaudible, until the vacuum cleaner was switched off, when she would open her eyes wider and clearly demand to know why you had stopped.

Tiny, nine months her senior and now a healthy, albeit still very small cat, loved Tabitha dearly, though sometimes she felt the need to pull this ebullient, effervescent show-off down to earth.

Thanks to Tabitha I was doing a great deal of showing of cats, making many new friends and enjoying it almost as much as she did; but my breeding was getting nowhere.

My two white females, both booked into aristocratic males, showed no signs of breeding. Gussie, beautiful friendly Gussie, no longer looked beautiful. Her round face looked strangely drawn, she was cross and surly with all - human or feline - and she had recurring bouts of eczema. Finally the vet diagnosed cystic ovaries and suggested spaying as the only cure. As soon as she began to recover from the operation the change in her was dramatic, in fact so much so that the vet, whose name was Thylor, always made a joke of her when he saw her after that, saying, 'Now that's what I call a "tailor- made" cat!'

She lived until she was seventeen, another ten years, and I don't remember a single day's illness from then on. But of course there were no more kittens, aristocat or alley cat, white or brown.

I began to wonder if I would ever have any kittens from Tiny. At eighteen months old she had shown no sign of being in season, or 'calling'. When she finally did and was despatched to a handsome aristocat on the other side of London, she was returned under a cloud three days later - unmated. I was told when I obeyed the peremptory telegram from the stud owner to phone her, that she had been so ferocious that she had absolutely terrified poor Nlmrod.

I was so relieved to learn that no harm had befallen my precious little cat and so amused at the image of Tiny, all six pounds of her, terrifying the magnificent stud cat, who must have been at least twice her weight, that I laughed aloud. Not long after that he was retired from public stud. I wondered if maybe my diminutive odd-eyed virago, so fiercely defending her virtue, had given him some dreadful psychological hang-up!

I decided to mate her with old Tim, Tabitha's father, who was now registered. Meanwhile Tabitha had been sent away to be mated to a very aristocratic Red Tabby, there being no suitable Brown available within reasonable distance. From this union I could reasonably expect Brown Tabbies, Red Tabbies, and maybe the odd Tortoiseshell.

Many years later, after I was married, I had a true aristocat. Honey was an elegant Abyssinian, a breed believed by many to be the same cat as those worshipped along the Nile so many thousands of years ago. Certainly Ancient Egyptian papyrus paintings portray cats remarkably like present-day Abyssinians.

Honey too was a delight, in many ways so like my fun-loving Tabitha that it was almost as if I had her back again in different form: she too loved shows and showing off. She had a glorious sense of fun and devised many crazy games, just as Tabitha did.

Both would retrieve, just like a dog - the only cats I have had do this. Throw a ball of screwed-up paper and they would race after it, leaping on or diving under any obstacle it landed on or under and carrying it back to me in their teeth to drop it at my feet.

Like Tabitha, Honey was a joy to show; such cats not only enjoy being shown but make showing enjoyable for their owners. I have had other cats who did not like being shown. Tiberius or Timmy - Tiny's son from her union with old Tim - was one such. He was a striking Brown Tabby with the most fabulous eyes. Large and round, they were the wonderful aquamarine of a Chinchilla. It was for all the world as if the blue of Tiny's one brilliant blue eye had been mixed, like paint, with the lemon colour of old Tim's eyes to produce the colour of their son's eyes. I showed him just enough to get the coveted Ch. for Champion in front of his name, then retired him; though he behave~ well, it was all too obvious that unlike his ebullient half-sister and subsequent mate Tabitha, he did not enjoy it at all.

Candy, a beautiful white daughter of Tiny's from a later mating with a British Blue, was not so well-behaved. Showing Candy was beset with hazards. On one never-to-be-forgotten occasion she escaped from me as I handed her over to the vet for the usual pre-show examination and headed off towards the entrance of the huge horticultural hall in Westminster, London. I went after her, with the visions of my precious puss rushing out into the streets of London, ne'er to be seen again!

When she ignored the open doors and headed down the stairs to the basement instead, I almost wished I never need see her again, for the only thing down those stairs was the men's toilets. Fortunately she had never liked men, so when she got there she turned round and headed back up the stairs where I managed to fling myself on her before she shot past me again.

After this traumatic beginning to the day, or perhaps because of it, she behaved quite disgracefully. I came back to the hall after lunch not to find her pen covered with prize cards as I hoped (and expected, for she was truly a beautiful cat)', but Candy purring loudly and beaming in truly Cheshire-cat fashion at an admiring member of the public.

Only one card adorned her pen and on it was written the shameful words: 'This cat is dangerous to handle. Do not judge'. I learned afterwards that having bitten the first judge of the day she was not thereafter judged in any of her many classes. I decided this was the time to retire Candy from the show pen.

Showing cats can be fun, and is much easier oil the handler than the exhibition of most other animals: nowadays one is not expected actually to handle one's own cat. In fact the owners are not even expected to be present during the judging.

Imagine the hassles in the early days of cat showing in England when the exhibits were led around on leashes in a small enclosure. This practice was stopped. Cats are not the easiest animals to train to walk on a leash, and are about the least reliable even when they are trained. Particularly large virile males! It was the bad behaviour of the stud cats, that is, the entire males, that changed the method of showing.

For the serious breeder of pedigree cats, the show pen is his shop window and a very necessary form of advertising, particularly if they have a male cat at stud. For my part I enjoyed the time I spent showing and made many new friends. I found a good deal less 'bitchiness' in the world of pedigree cats than in many other competitive circles in the animal world.

I think the point at which the showing of any type of animal becomes objectionable is when individual animals become of value only because of their show successes; when physical excellence in the animals becomes the all-important feature in the breeder's mind; and also when the competitive spirit that exists in all of us takes over to the exclusion of genuine love for the animals and feelings of friendship towards other exhibitors.

The majority of cat breeders, I found, really cared for their animals, and the majority of show cats lived happy lives. I would also say that the greater number of the kittens bred eventually found their way to good homes.

People who actually go out and buy a kitten usually really want it and are therefore prepared to give it a good home. At least, that was the assumption I worked on, and doing so I was able to convince myself that not only was I thoroughly enjoying my involvement in the world of pedigree cats, but I was doing my particular cats a good turn too. For by elevating their status from that of alley cat to aristo cat I had created a demand for them.

Occasionally the thought flitted into my mind that maybe all I was really doing was pandering to the snobbery inherent in us, and that catdom as a whole was not really benefitting at all. when such thoughts did enter my head I did not allow them to linger, but it is a thorny question, and I am still not sure of the answer. Do the breeders of pedigree cats enhance the lot of all cats by raising their status, making people aware of them, by breeding cats of rare and excellent beauty that are much in demand? Or do they merely compound the appalling problem of the millions of unloved, uncared-for, unwanted cats destined to have miserable and usually short lives? I really don't know.

What I do know is that aristocats, once you get to know them, are really no different from alley cats; it is their circumstances, not their pedigrees that make them different. The humblest moggy will become as haughty as the champion show winner once he can get himself established in a suitable home with the right type of human - that is, one willing and eager to treat him as an aristo-cat!

Chapter 4
Learning from Cats

To many people, the idea that our animal friends have anything to teach us borders on the absurd. I think man has much to learn from other species that inhabit this earth with him - and our friend the cat is perhaps the greatest guru of them all.

Today we are all very much aware of stress - not just in our own lives, but through the media. We know how much illness is stress-related. With the spread of 'New Age' thinking many people are moving away from the idea of relieving stress with drugs and looking for better ways. Meditation groups, courses and books abound, and relaxation classes are held in almost every community.

Many people who attend these courses and classes share their home with someone who knows more about the art of true relaxation and meditation than most of us can hope to learn in a lifetime - their cat.

The hunting cat can certainly teach us singleness of purpose, and patience; but though when stalking her prey she can wait for hours on end, apparently oblivious of cold and even damp, with every muscle and nerve poised and tense, she can also relax totally, from her whiskers to her claws.

Any one who has been to classes or listened to a tape on relaxation will be familiar with the instructions to work from the tips of the toes to the top of the head, or the top of the head to the tips of the toes, and slowly relax each set of muscles as, one comes to them. The cat would appear to have mastered the art of doing this automatically and even that of totally relaxing her body in one hit. My present Tabitha can relax so perfectly that she can sit, legs dangling. In the palm of my son's outstretched hand; she is an average to large cat for a female, so this is no mean feat.

Glorious extrovert that she is, she has no inhibitions and I often find her in strange positions, rather like a rag doll that has been carelessly flung down, sometimes on her back with arms akimbo. If I put my finger under a front paw, I usually find the claws are retracted and the muscles so relaxed that the paw can be gently 'flipped'.

There are few happy mediums in Tabitha's life: she is either asleep, awake but in a state of total relaxation, or awake and full of demonic energy - her batteries fully charged.

What, I often think, could 1 achieve if only I had half her energy? Before I can hope for that I must learn how to achieve something akin to her state of relaxation. I'm working on it - with her help.

Una is a charming elderly lady who shares her apartment with an equally charming Smoke Persian cat. She and I had been attending a meditation course together.

'Do you know', she said to me, 'each time I meditate I find my cat sitting with me. At first I thought it was just coincidence; now I think he's meditating with me!'

We intellectual humans are apt to equate intelligence and learning with wisdom. This is a great mistake. Wisdom is an in-built in-knowing added to by experience. It is not something that can be put on a person like education or intellectual achievement. These latter may add to a person's wisdom quotient. but there is no certainty they will.

In fact I am sure we can all cite instances of people who have great mental and scholastic achievements yet can appear perfect idiots when it comes to the ordering of their day-to-day lives.

The majority of cats seem born with a store of in-built or inherent wisdom which can be exhibited by quite young kittens. Cats spend so much of their time meditating (or, as Rosaleen Norton says, operating on the astral plane while they are here in the physical) that surely they must, if only we could learn, have much to teach us about that side of life? The following story was given to me by a cat-loving friend, and is told here in her own words.

This story is about a cat that once owned us in the days of my youth. Her name was Prudence and she was very much part of the family. She liked to preside over family activities from the padded high back of a tall armchair that had been inherited from a great-grandmother. From this perch she would watch through amused, half-slit eyes the high jinks of a predominantly teenage family.

One day it came about that a seance was mooted as entertainment for the evening. After the table had been cleared and the elders were seen to be safely ensconced in the lounge several rooms up the hall to listen to radio and read (TV was still a thing of the future), we set up our crude apparatus.

We chalked the alphabet, a set of numbers and the words 'yes' and 'no' in a circle around the table. Then with the lights subdued with drapes and a tumbler turned upside down, we set forth to call in 'someone' from the 'other side'.

We tried, 'Is anyone there?' without result. Then we named a few famous people like Nellie Melba and Captain Cook. Then someone suggested we should be trying to contact someone we knew, such as Aunt Babs, who had died in her sleep a few years previously. or the boy who had drowned in the school pool when we were all still at primary school, or the grandfather we had all adored as little children, but whose memory was now mere tracery in our minds. But this seemed to be getting a bit scary, and there were elements of disrespect, so we quickly abandoned it. It was decided to try to contact a family member we knew well by tradition only, and great-grandmother was the logical candidate. She had passed on a good generation or so before we were born but she had been a matriarch of the first order and had left an indelible blueprint for family behaviour that we youngsters had spent many years trying to reform.

We boldly exclaimed her name and placed our hands firmly on the glass. It began to move. We all yiped in shivery anticipation. Our spokeswoman asked in a squeaky voice: 'Is that you great-grandma?' The glass started to have a life of its own. It slid this way and that on the polished table, making fantastic shadows in the dim light.

Suddenly there was a wild scream from the other side of the room and Prudence carne flying down from her perch right onto the centre of the table. She scattered our outstretched arms and sent the glass shooting onto the carpet, whence it rolled harmlessly right under the sideboard.

That really ended proceedings. The oldies were already treading down the hall and we barely had time to restore the light, throw the big tapestry cloth across the table and reach for the playing cards. Anyway, we were cowards, all of us.

In retrospect I do not for one moment think that we had ventured into a case of transmigration or anything like that, but we were all pretty well convinced that Prudence knew more about seances than we did and she broke it up before we got too involved.

Cats of course are remarkable teachers of their own young, particularly in the matter of all-important survival skills. Dear old Muggins would systematically teach her children how to hunt. A fantastic and intrepid ratter herself, in the normal course of events she never made the mistake of overfacing her kittens by presenting them with a rat when they were babies but always started them off on really small fry, tiny mice scarcely from the nest. First she would bring freshly killed ones and present them as a toy or plaything. Then a mouse a little bit larger, and still alive, would be brought, and so on.

When she had kittens, and only then, she would go off on rabbiting excursions and always bring back a nice young rabbit which she would skin in the most skilful way for them to eat.

I do not think Muggins had always found life easy before she came to live with us. She knew what it was to have to survive on her own and she was determined her children should have the necessary skills to enable them to do likewise should the need arise. There is a very good indirect lesson here too for us as human parents. The very essence of good parenting, surely, is to bring up our children to be self-reliant and able to look after themselves in the world, to see that they have the necessary skills to enable them to be independent.

Perhaps the time when Muggins took her kittens off, nearly a couple of miles, and kept them on rabbits until my father found them a fortnight later and brought them back, was a lesson in survival for them, or a reminder and reassurance to herself that she could survive without human help. Or perhaps she was teaching us a lesson - that we did not own her, that she lived with us because she chose to? Maybe it was a blend of all these.

Cats, I think, have much to teach us in the matter of personal relationships. They have a capacity for deep affection, loyalty and devotion, but they know how to give their love and still live their own individual private lives, and let you - as the object of their love - live yours. How many of us can do the same? When we love we want to possess, too often not only the time but also the thoughts of the loved one.

They really appreciate the quality of a cat's love and companionship, it is probably necessary to live quite alone with a cat as I did for some time with Tiny. Never once did I return home without a gentle greeting of real pleasure and affection. She gave me perfect companionship without in any way demanding my company. In fact, looking back I feel I took far more from her than I gave in return.

There are many small personal lessons to be learned from the cat. Fastidious both about food (not for her anything going slightly off) and her personal appearance. No other animal spends so much time cleaning itself and making sure it always presents a clean and tidy appearance to the world. This grooming process may even be extended to a loved human, as many people who have experienced the rough edge of a cat's tongue will know!

The cat's tongue does indeed have a rough edge, rather like a small brush, and is designed to clean each hair perfectly.

The cat would appear to have a rudimentary sense of plumbing with her habit of digging neat little 'toilets' and carefully filling them after use. It is this trait that makes it possible to keep a cat in a flat without its ever going outside. One simply provides it with a tray filled with earth, ashes, sawdust or some other 'diggable' material in a discreet corner. Special trays and absorbent litter for the purpose can be purchased at most pet stores. Even the tiniest kitten can be taught to use a tray; but they do expect your cooperation in the matter of regularly changing and keeping it clean.

Some cats have such an advanced idea of plumbing that they will use a human toilet! In my cat-showing days back in

England I used to stay with a fellow cat breeder in London when I took my cats to shows in the Big Smoke. Mary bred very beautiful British Blues - blue cats with short coats, round faces and round deep amber eyes. One of these regularly used the WC. It is quite an astonishing sight to find a cat carefully straddling (one hind and one front foot each side) the seat of a toilet you are just about to use yourself!

I never had a cat who actually did this, but Candy, one of Tiny's daughters, regularly used the plughole of the bath to urinate down (positioning herself very carefully so that her aim was accurate!) when she shared a London flat with me. She gave this up when we left London and returned to the country and she could go outside. I must say I did nothing to discourage this habit as it was so much easier to turn the bath tap on and 'flush' the plughole than it was to change a cat tray!

Cats have many other qualities that we like to think of as virtues in the human character. They have a patience and single-mindedness of purpose when hunting that would surely get any human being to the very top of their particular professional tree.

They are usually very punctual, and expect you to be the same. If breakfast is at eight, lunch at one and dinner at seven, then those are the times they will turn up and expect to be served.

Cats are often castigated for selfishness. But are they so much selfish and self-centred as self sufficient and self reliant? Even the most spoilt and pampered pet puss can, when need be, look after herself extraordinarily well. Sheba, most delicate and apparently helpless of all my cats, has proved this to me when she has returned after several days off, I know not where, in fine fettle.

Trading on this ability to look after number one and using it to square their own consciences, callous cat owners dump their unwanted cats in the bush.

More often than not the cat, with her remarkable ability to adapt and change from domestic pet to wild animal, survives - and even thrives. If not de-sexed (and few dumped cats are, for caring owners who make sure this is done do not usually subsequently abandon their cats to their fate), they can not only thrive but breed. Thus we have the problem of feral cats - which are not genuine wild cats such as the Scottish wild cat, but domestic cats gone wild - with their tragic effects on the genuine wildlife of the bush, the birds and small fauna. Those who dump cats are showing an irresponsibility that the cat herself would never display.

Abandoning cats the other way round, that is taking country cats and 'losing' them in the city is, from the cats' point of view, even more callous and certainly, again from the cats' angle, more disastrous. While the nature of the cat is such that she can usually revert very quickly to the wild, it is far harder for a cat brought up in the freedom and space of the country to survive in the city. Only a very small percentage will be lucky enough to end up on a friendly doorstep with 'welcome' on the mat. Some will inevitably be victims of traffic, others of hunger and disease. The best they can hope for is a merciful end.

The habit of dumping unwanted animals is not only irresponsible, but quite irreconcilable with any standard of ethics, Christian or otherwise, and certainly makes us ponder on the so called superiority of man in the animal world.

What makes it so appalling is that it is totally unnecessary. If all cat owners had their kittens desexed as a matter of routine, there would be very, very few unwanted cats. Failing this obvious and simple course, there are veterinary surgeons and animal welfare societies everywhere who will destroy unwanted animals humanely. The cat's personal tragedy is that she is too prolific. If only female cats had one kitten every two years, instead of two litters of four to six kittens a year, the heartache of so many surplus cats would no longer exist.

Dana as a tiny kitten with the pup Zoe

Abandoning a grown cat is harsh enough, but 'throwing away' totally helpless baby kittens shows a cool disregard for suffering that is quite spine-chilling.

I had been to Sydney for a couple of days, seen off at the station in the city by Ruth, my cat-loving seventeen-year-old daughter. When I got back I was met at our local station by my son. 'Ruth's got another cat,' he told me as we drove home. 'What!' I exclaimed. We already had six cats, which seemed like a full complement. 'Where did she get it from? She hasn't bought another? What is it like?'

Graham only smiled enigmatically. 'Wait till you see it,' was all he would say. His lips, it seemed, were sealed. As we drove home I was inwardly fuming. The last addition to the family, number six, was Kit, whom Ruth had actually bought in a pet shop. I could see the entire home being taken over by cats if she was going to keep on like this!

I remembered what a load of trouble Kit had brought into the family, after Ruth, wandering as if drawn by a magnet into the pet shop, had obeyed the kitten's command to 'buy me'. A few days after her arrival in the household, she was a very sick kitten indeed with enteritis: the beginning of what seemed an interminable period of cleaning up after her and watching her shrink instead of grow! Then, just as she seemed to be getting out of the wood, a bald patch on her ear, a circular bald patch, turned out to be ringworm. It spread to other parts of her body, to Lucy, one of Ruth's other cats, and to Ruth herself.

Ruth met me with the new 'cat' in her hand. It was too small to hold in her arms. A tiny scrap of blotched tabby fur, she looked boldly at me, and the rest of the world, with slate- blue baby eyes, scarcely able to focus. She was far too young to leave her mother, scarcely old enough to survive away from her even with loving care.

My prepared protest died on my lips. 'Wherever did you find her?' I asked. Ruth told me that when she left me at the station to walk back into the town she heard a terrible screaming. 'I had to go and see what it was.'

'Of course'. I nodded, knowing full well that one sound Ruth could not resist was that of a cat in distress.

'There was Dana' (she had already given her a name); 'I was amazed when I saw such a tiny creature making all that noise!'

Now that we know Dana better, it does not seem amazing at all. Dana is tough through and through, with the strongest instinct for survival I have ever seen. I am sure that when she saw Ruth coming, that instinct must have urged her to put everything she had into making her hear.

She has never shown fear of anything or anyone, but asserted herself in the house almost at once in a way that seemed quite incredible for such a small creature. I feel that her mother must have imparted in her the firm conviction that when there was food around you ate - and ate - because you never knew when it would be around again! So small she could be held in the palm of the hand, she would growl with incredible ferocity over her own food and look the older cats squarely in the eye as she calmly took theirs. She has no fear whatsoever of the dogs, but plays with the twitching paw of Heidi, the elderly German Shepherd, as she dozes, smacks Ginger the Poodle firmly on the nose, and wrestles with Zoe the adolescent terrier till she begs for mercy.

As Dana grows, her strong survival instinct is burgeoning into an enormous zest for life. Whether she is being the intrepid hunter stalking the guinea-fowl rooster through the tall summer grass, playing rough-and-tumble games with Zoe or Kit, or purring full throttle beneath a caressing hand, she is doing it with 'zing'. The lesson she is teaching is that life is good - it is for living, and enjoying!

I believe that our life here on this earth is one long learning experience. If the time ever comes that we cease to learn, then we no longer exist. Learning is living, and it is a continuous process. Every creature that we come in contact with, that touches our lives in any way, has something to offer. The deepest and most important lessons may just as well be taught by a little kitten as the wisest sage.

Dana Grown Up

Chapter 5
Family Life

*-But the wildest of all the wild animals was the Cat. He
walked by himself and all places were alike to him.*

Rudyard Kipling

Cats and family life are not usually associated. Kipling's cat
(from Just-So Stories) makes his bargain with the Woman but
insists, to the infuriation of the Man, that he will remain the
cat who 'walked by himself and all places were alike to him';
he refuses to 'belong' to the family - even though, In typical cat
manner, he has managed to become almost symbolic of cosy
home life.

Neither does the picture of the cat walking alone, rather than
in a pack like the dog, call to mind visions of the cat as a
'family man' within his own species. Yet cats become very
much a part of the human family circle, on their own terms of
course, and often have a warm and close-knit family life of
their own.

'Family' does not necessarily mean the modern conventional
nuclear family of mother, father and offspring. It can be any
assorted group who choose to live together as a group and thus
form a family. I often talk about my 'family of cats' (seven
members at the time of writing), yet not one is related by blood
to another.

Tiny and Tabitha became such close friends that they almost
formed a family on their own. When they both had kittens
within ten days of each other the group was very definitely a
family.

Both litters turned out to be very much a surprise packet, but especially Tabitha's four: all were some sort of blue! - and this from a brown Tabby mother and a Champion Red Tabby father. Not so entirely amazing as it may seem to anyone with a knowledge both of breeding show cats and cat genetics. Blue cats usually excel in both type and eye colour and therefore breeders of other colours often cross to them to improve the quality of their stock. Genetically blue is a recessive gene and therefore the progeny are not usually that colour. However if this gene is carried by both parents the progeny, or some of them, will be blue.

The handsome red champion I knew had blue in his ancestry. I had no idea Tabitha did, so I was very surprised when the litter I expected to consist of Brown or Red Tabbies and possibly Tortoiseshell females all turned out in the dilute form of these colours, that is blue. The most unusual and handsome of them all, a Blue Tabby, was dead at birth, or squashed at birth. I was never quite sure which, as I was not present when Tabitha's kittens were actually born and she was such a frivolous haphazard creature. Blue Tabbies were once a very popular variety but virtually died out. They are very pretty cats, the coat striped and patterned in two shades of blue or grey, quite different from the Silver Tabby, which has black markings on a ground coat of the palest silver.

One of the females was very similar in colour, except that she had patches of red blurring the pattern, an inheritance from her red father. The other female was a perfect Blue Cream, that is blue and cream in patches. This colour is the dilute form of Tortoiseshell, which is red and black in patches. The surviving male was plain blue. I called them Shot Silk, Matilda and Just William and duly registered them with my prefix.

Tabitha produced her family without any fuss and looked after them in much the same manner. When the novelty had worn off (within a few hours) she seemed to find motherhood one crashing bore, spending the minimum time with her family and the rest about her own business.

Not so Tiny. Ten days after Tabitha's kittens were born I was awakened just after midnight by Tiny sitting on the bed, patting my face with her paw and yowling. From that moment on sleep was impossible. Tiny had no intention of having her kittens without me present and fully conscious. Just before dawn I was allowed to drop off into an exhausted sleep as Tiny, purring in satisfaction, curled in a small white crescent around four beautiful chubby kittens. Three were white, all with the smudge-mark guarantee of perfect hearing, and one was a perfectly marked Brown Tabby.

The reaction of my two little cats to motherhood was totally different, proving that cats are as much individuals as anybody else and disproving the oft-quoted theory that animals are only good mothers by instinct.

Tiny was a much better mother because she was a much more serious personality, but instinct seemed to have let her down badly. For the first three days she had no idea about cleaning up the kittens and was very disturbed when they soiled the bed. For the first time I began to wonder what sort of a cat mother she had had; perhaps after all it was not entirely her human owner who had been responsible for the terrible undernourished condition she was in when I acquired her. She learned how to clean them up and thereafter kept them scrupulously clean in every way. Neither did she have the vaguest notion of how to move her kittens. While Tabitha was forever picking up her kittens and putting them somewhere else, Tiny never did and when she had to move them to another part of the bed she did it by pushing or pulling them with her paw.

Tabitha, always an opportunist, took full advantage of this and also of Tiny's more conscientious attitude to motherhood. When she wanted to go off and leave her family she would pick them all up and dump them in Tiny's bed, confident that Tiny would look after them in her absence, however prolonged.

This was all very well, but occasionally when she came back after some interesting excursion she would decide to take all seven kittens back to her bed; poor Tiny, who had no idea how to carry hers back again, would peer into Tabitha's bed, then gaze at me demanding that I do something!

All seven kittens eventually went out into the world although Blanche, one of Tiny's daughters, had several adventures before she was finally settled. I sold her first as a pet to some people who brought her back three days later because their child was mauling her! Hadn't I, they asked, got a cheaper kitten they could have, which wouldn't matter!

Appalled, I took Blanche back, gave them their money and the advice to buy a stuffed cat if they couldn't control their child!

Blanche was in such a traumatic state, spending most of her waking hours in the next few weeks under the furniture, that I didn't try to sell her again but decided to keep her. I took her to Bristol Cat Show - when she had recovered her nerve, where she won several prizes and a photograph was taken of her which eventually appeared in The Observers' Book of Cats. I also showed her at the National Cat Show in the vast Olympia Hall in London. Like her half-sister, Tabitha, she enjoyed shows. When she was six months old, 1 had a letter from some people in the Isle of Man who particularly wanted a white cat but could only get Manx cats there. After much correspondence to convince me that this really would be a good (and childless) home, I agreed to sell her. She was despatched by rail to Liverpool, where a representative of the RSPCA met her and put her on the plane for Douglas. Her new owners phoned me immediately they got her home and said she stepped out of her travelling box purring.

William, Tabitha's Boy Blue, really fell on his paws. He went at eight weeks old to a truly wonderful home and came back to board each year when his owners went away, travelling out in state, the only passenger in a taxi for the eight-mile ride.

Tiny's other two white kittens also went to excellent homes - the male, Crackerjack to become the dearly loved pet of a lonely little girl, Colette to the well-known artist Vere Temple. Tiberlus, or Tim, I kept as a husband for Tabitha. He grew up to be a most striking-looking and lovable cat with his wonderful sable-and-black coat and his fantastic aquamarine eyes; he was also more like Tiny than any of her white kittens!

It was a happy decision. Not only did he quickly become a champion, but he and Tabitha really did form a most affectionate relationship and Tim became quite a 'family man', developing a paternal feeling towards his kittens that is very rare in male cats.

In fact he showed a good deal more patience and tolerance with them than Tabitha, allowing them to crawl all over him pulling his whiskers and ears and pouncing on his tall, which he obligingly switched and twitched for them.

Hitherto I had always thought of Tabbies as 'ordinary' cats: not any more. There was nothing ordinary about my beautiful brownies. They won prize cards whenever shown and were much in demand, kittens often being sold even before they were born. I sent them all over England and one even went to Scotland, back to the land of her grandmother. How strange that my attempts to breed white cats should end in my becoming a successful breeder of Brown Tabbies!

Tiny had two more litters by a very aristocratic champion Shorthair Blue cat. The first time she had two white males and a black female; the second litter was exactly the same except that she reversed the sexes, two white females and a black male!

Since all these whites had yellow eyes, albeit more orange than lemon thanks to their father with his deep orange eyes, and I was still dreaming of a blue- eyed white, I sold them. However, Candy, the better of the two females, who went to a breeder in Devon, was eventually to return to me, physically fit, but psychologically a wreck. Had I known that Tiny would never have any more kittens, I would never have sold her in the first place.

We had in our cat family at the time one of the few cats I have ever disliked in my life. He was a plain black-and-white known as Bertie. He was a thoroughly mean and bullying character and Tiny, being so much smaller than him, was a prime target. One day when she was trotting down the garden path after me he appeared, from nowhere it seemed, and pounced on her. As he bowled her over she hit her head on the corner of a brick which was used as part of the ornamental edging to a flowerbed.

For a moment she lay still, then she got up, obviously dazed; her head wobbled and she keeled over. I carried her Inside. In the house she reeled about as if drunk or recovering from a general anaesthetic. Half an hour later when she was still doing this and vomiting I phoned the vet.

He guessed that her sense of balance had been upset and it was that which was causing the vomiting. He advised me to keep her as still and quiet as I could. I spent every minute I could with her. I shut her in the travelling box when I had to leave her, for she was being a danger to herself- trying to get on chairs and keeling off them, lurching perilously close to the open fire.

The next day she was no better and I took her into the vet. After examining her he told me that her eardrum was damaged. There was nothing that he could do but, hopefully, she would gradually learn to compensate for It. If not ...

The alternative implied by that 'if not' did not bear contemplation. Sadly I took her home and once more caring for my beloved and oh so frail little white cat became all-consuming; in her new dependence on me the already close bond between us grew even closer.

The vet was right. She did learn to compensate; the vomiting ceased and eventually she could walk and even run. But for the remainder of her life her head was always tilted to one side and if she were pushed or even put down suddenly her precarious command of her balance momentarily left her, her head shook and sometimes she even fell over. The vet advised me to have her spayed. I knew it was sound advice. How could this pathetically frail scrap of cat stand up to the train journey to a stud cat, mating and subsequent bearing and rearing of kittens? With a heavy heart I agreed - wondering also how she would stand the operation!

But he was an understanding vet; he knew that the bond between us was unusually close.

'I want you,' he said 'to have her at my surgery at nine o'clock. Normally I like to keep them here for the first night after the operation, but I feel she will be much better if she can come round at home. Will you please be here to fetch her home no later than 11.30? That should give her time to get home before she comes out of the anaesthetic.'

I did as he asked and sat by her, metaphorically holding her hand as she struggled to regain consciousness in much the same way that I had been with her when she had her kittens.

From then on Tiny and I were virtually inseparable. Never for one moment did I regret my purchase of her; she was such a wonderful companion. But with her spayed, my dream of breeding white cats with forget-me-not-blue eyes and perfect hearing had to be consigned to the limbo of lost dreams.

There was no shortage of kittens though, for beautiful batty Tabitha still went on having kittens. She grew no more serious about motherhood as the years rolled by and Tiny often found herself pressed into service as 'kitten-sitter'.

Sometimes our efforts to form a 'family' unit in cats can fail miserably A year or so ago my husband brought home a delightful tabby-and-white kitten which we called Lucy A couple of weeks later we were asked by some neighbours if we would like a kitten from their beautiful Siamese-Burmese female. Our first reaction was no; we had just got a new kitten.

'Two kittens aren't really much more trouble than one,' my husband remarked as Lucy ripped wildly round the house in some mad kitten game.

'They can sometimes be less,' I agreed. 'They amuse each other.'

And so Tabitha the second joined the family ostensibly as a 'little sister' for Lucy at first all was harmony The two kittens ate, slept and played together, happily sharing a bed in the bathroom. But as they grew and their personalities unfolded things changed.

The first thing we noticed was that they were no longer sharing the comfy bed in the bathroom. If you went in the bathroom after they had gone to bed for the night, invariably Tabitha was curled up happily in the bed. Lucy, not quite so happily, would be sleeping, or trying to sleep, on the top of the laundry basket.

My daughter solved that problem by promoting Lucy to her bedroom. Then we noticed they were quarrelling over their food. One day the peace of a sunny summer afternoon was shattered by two cats yowling and fighting. Two visiting toms? Surely not - all our cats were neutered.

We ran them to earth and found no visiting toms, only Tabitha bailing up Lucy in a corner of the sun-deck. And so it went on. Only once did Lucy come out on top, and that was when they both went to the vet to be spayed. Lucy came back spry as a spring chicken, apparently feeling little or no ill effects. Not so Tabitha. For twenty-four hours her legs refused to support her and even her raucous Siamese voice was reduced to a thin croak.

Now they are both grown-up cats, Lucy keeps out of Tabitha's way whenever she can and no doubt curses the day we had kind ideas about giving her a 'sister'. Tabitha teases Lucy and chases her and bullies and threatens her whenever she thinks no one is around to stop her. So much for human interference!

We have always shared our home with a family of cats ranging in number from as few as one, when we first arrived in Australia from England and brought Tilly with us, to as many as eight or nine.

I have noticed that there is a definite hierarchy or 'pecking order' among them, the boss cat usually being the oldest. Just how strong an influence this cat exerts is not always obvious until they are no longer there.

When dear old Lottie died, it seemed that anarchy reigned supreme in our cat family Lottie was Tilly's daughter; born in Tasmania, she moved with us to Victoria and then again into two more homes with us. She was an unusual and beautiful cat, shorthaired and round faced, a rich sable colour with tabby markings on her head and a ticked body coat, rather like an Abyssinian. She was also very like a possum and people often told me that is what I should have called her. But I called her Lottie because, when she was born, she was spotted rather than ticked.

'Oh, you are a spotty Lottie!' I had said when I first held her in my hand, and the name stuck.

In spite of being very frail and sick for the last few years of her life (she lived until she was twelve), Lottie was never bullied by the other cats. 'Mind over matter, 'we would say But it wasn't until she was dead that we realised just how strong her influence really was over the other cats. For two or three months after her death, there was constant strife among the cats. Those who had got on perfectly amicably before were now scrapping.

Then gradually it seemed a new boss cat was emerging - Fluffy, a blue-cream longhair, my daughter's special friend and next in seniority. Gradually, as she assumed her position, relative peace and harmony prevailed. Even Tabitha learned to behave herself when Fluffy was around!

Fluffy, though a relatively small cat, has a haughty mien and flashing eyes, she reminds me of the Martial Marigold in the poem by Richard Garnett who

Moved through the garden in glory because She had very long claws at the end of her paws.

Fluffy does not mind using her very long claws on cat, dog or person if she thinks their behaviour warrants it!

We humans, I sometimes think, lay far too much stress on instinct and far too little on learning when we are dealing with animals. Dealing with our own species we probably lay equally too much stress the other way round. The following sad, but unfortunately true story illustrates this all too well.

A woman was walking through the park with her children when one of them picked up something alive from the grass. It was a kitten, so new its eyes were not even open. They were all, mother and children, touched by its fragility and helplessness. They took it home. Devotedly and painstakingly, the woman reared it, feeding it first with an eye-dropper until at last it began to lap for itself. It was an ordinary little cat, just plain black and white with nothing to recommend it greatly and one great disadvantage. It was female.

However one day a friend visited with her seven- year-old daughter. The child fell in love with the kitten and begged for it. Believing it would have a good home, the original rescuer let it go. Unfortunately the kitten did not know that It was supposed to transfer Its love and devotion to the child; torn abruptly from the only home and 'mother' it had known, it did not take kindly to its new role of plaything. The child soon grew bored with it and the mother, who hadn't really wanted it anyway kept it on sufferance.

All might still have been well if it had been spayed, but alas, she was allowed to have kittens.

With no memories of her own cat mother and thus no example of how to rear kittens to follow, she simply did not know what to do with them. She and her kittens made the one-way trip to the vet that is the fate of so many unwanted cats. What a tragic end for a cat who at one point in her life had been the focal point of so much love and care! And how unnecessary.

Now that I no longer either breed pedigree cats or even keep an unspayed cat as a pet, we no longer have cat families in the sense that we have litters of kittens, but this certainly does not mean that the cats do not form a family unit among themselves and also with members of the human family

My daughter has three special cats of her own which, together with Ruth herself, form a family unit within the family Similarly other cats have special ties with other members of the family.

It is one of the many strange paradoxes of the cat that while she is still, and always will be, 'the cat who walks by herself', she is also the living symbol of home, hearth and family life.

As E.V Lucas neatly put it:

> *A kitten frisking by the fire*
> *Is every proper man's desire.*

The addition of a kitten can often make a couple a family, a house a home.

Chapter 6
Nine Lives?

- They will come back, come back again,
as long as the red Earth rolls.
He never wasted a leaf or a tree.
Do you think he would squander souls?

Rudyard Kipling

There is a well-known story about a little Hindu boy who, when asked in school to write about his favourite animal, chose to write on the cat. In his essay he wrote: 'The cat has nine lives - except in Europe where it only has one because of Christianity'. He may have been a bit confused about the significance (in this instance) of the cat's nine lives but he certainly made a telling point about reincarnation.

Arthur Schopenhauer the nineteenth-century German philosopher, said more or less the same thing when he wrote:

Were an Asiatic to ask me for a definition of Europe, I should be forced to answer him: it is that part of the world which is haunted by the incredible delusion that man was created out of nothing, and that his present birth is his first entrance into life.

We who live in European-derived cultures, in whatever geographical portion of the globe, put a connotation on the common expression that a cat has nine lives quite different from that of the little Hindu boy. We judge it to mean that the cat has an inborn ability to escape unscathed from accidents and mishaps that would claim the lives of 'lesser' creatures.

When Tilly, the beloved black-and-white moggy who came out to Australia from England with us, was run over and left for dead at the side of the road just before we left England, the vet commented that had she been a dog or a person, she would almost certainly have been killed, but as she was a cat she had a fifty-fifty chance.

In true cat character she made good use of that chance and not only survived to come out to Australia but eventually made a complete recovery. Poor Tilly was however always accident-prone. This in fact was her second brush with death on the roads. The first time we were just finishing breakfast when John answered a knock on the back door. A young man stood there holding in his hands what certainly appeared to be a dead cat - Tilly. Behind him, weeping copiously, stood a young girl.

The young man told my husband that as they approached our drive gate Tilly ran out and was hit by the car in front, which did not stop. The caring young couple however were cat people themselves. They stopped, collected the 'body' and came to tell us what had happened.

John reached out to take her, but as he did so she quite literally sprang to life and raced off to hide among the bushes in the garden.

The girl's tears stopped flowing and they all gaped in amazement. When I found Tilly afterwards the only damage I could see was a tiny speck of blood on one ear. But I knew that was one life less.

She was only eight years old when she died, the victim of poison. Always an intrepid rabbiter wherever she lived, she had lost another life along the way when caught in a trap in Tasmania. She met her Nemesis when she caught a rabbit that must have just picked up the merciless 10:80 poison.

Perhaps we should not blithely assume that we are completely right and the little Hindu boy wrong in our interpretation of the cat's nine lives. Maybe after all the saying does refer to the many times a cat can return to this earth - as a cat. At least we can keep an open mind and take it as an ambiguous statement rather than certain fact.

I was recently making a phone call in a friend's busy office. Waiting for the number to answer I glanced from her cluttered desk and my attention was caught by the poster pinned above it on the wall. It was delightful, the picture of an infinitely appealing small kitten. But it was the words beneath that really grabbed me: 'Be good to me - this is only my first life!' An ambiguous statement with- the same double meaning as the saying about the cat's nine lives. Perhaps the anonymous writer meant it to be ambiguous - perhaps he, or she, meant us to think about the possibility of our feline friends having more than one life,. in the literal sense.

Vast numbers of the world's peoples since the dawn of history have believed in reincarnation. Many of them have also adhered to the doctrine of transmigration, or metempsychosis; that is, animal souls reincarnating again as humans and vice versa.

The Ancient Egyptian belief in this doctrine is shown in many of their carvings and paintings which show the ignominious return to earth in animal bodies of human souls that had been found wanting when, at death, they were weighed in the judgement scales before Osiris.

Whether or not one subscribes to this belief there can certainly be no punishment better fitted to the crime than for a person who had spent a lifetime exploiting or abusing animals to have to return to earth in the body of that particular creature. Perhaps too, for those who had spent an incarnation in unremitting toil in a human body, a lifetime as a pampered puss might be considered a just reward!

Pythagoras, who was said to have visited Egypt in his youth and been instructed by the priests in their religion, was a firm believer in the doctrine of transmigration and frequently warned his followers that souls never die but now inhabit one type of body, now another.

As wax may be stamped with various figures, melt and be stamped anew, yet always remain the same substance, so may the same soul appear in fresh likenesses. Therefore, if you bear love to your kindred, refrain, I entreat you, from violating the lives of those who may, perchance, be your relations.

The thought that the arrogant and haughty feline sharing your home is in reality one's equally arrogant and haughty Aunt Agnes who departed this life some years ago may be somewhat daunting. Even more daunting may be the prospect of spending one's next incarnation in feline form! Little wonder that, in the Western world at least, while reincarnation is gaining a degree of acceptance, most of us shy away from the idea of transmigration of souls.

Most of us find it quite easy to accept the idea of a sort of one-way transmigration, or what is often referred to as the evolution of the soul: animal souls 'growing' and evolving until they reach the stage where they can incarnate in human bodies.

Charles Leadbeater, one of the founders of the Theosophical movement, was a firm believer in this and at one time he had a cat which earned the greatest respect from all who knew it when he told them that it was in its last incarnation as an animal.

General Sir Thomas Edward Gordon in his autobiography, *A Varied Life*, published in 1906, told a delightful story of a man inhabiting the body of a cat.

In 1838, Sir Robert Grant, Governor of Bombay, died at Government House near Poona; on the evening of the day of his death a cat was seen to leave the house by the front door and walk up and down a particular path, just as the Governor had always done each evening at around sunset.

The Hindu sentry on duty observed this and it was immediately assumed that the soul of the deceased Governor had entered the body of one of the household cats. As there was some confusion which one it actually was, it was decided that any cat seen leaving Government House by the main door around sunset should be presumed to be the Governor and treated with due respect.

Consequently, General Sir Thomas Gordon related:

> *For twenty-five years an oral addition to the written standing orders of the native guard at Government House has been regularly communicated from one guard to another on relief: namely that any cat thus seen should be assumed to be the Governor and saluted accordingly. The order was accepted without question and the entire guard obeyed, 'presenting arms' to any cat that appeared around sunset.*

Even though we may not subscribe to the doctrine of transmigration, we often pay lip service to it. I have in my present-day cat family an adored feline lady of mixed ancestry, her mother a very lovely Siamese-Burmese, her father, alas, unknown.

Tabitha is a glorious extrovert who loves nothing better than socialising, showing off and having her photo taken - in fact, being admired. How often we have remarked that she must have been an actress, a film star, or something similar in her last life.

I am sure we are not alone in seeing human characteristics, or what we think of as human characteristics, in our animals and speculating on what they were last time around.

Deep down I probably think that Tabitha was just - Tabitha. What else, I sometimes wonder, could have prompted me to give her the name of the beautiful, lovable extrovert I had lived with nearly thirty years ago? At first sight there was nothing about her to remind me of that other much loved cat - she was not even the same breed, and in all those intervening years I had never once thought of calling one of the many kittens who shared them with me by that name. Yet when my younger son Max asked, 'What shall we call her?', I found myself suggesting, 'Tabitha?'.

Even more strange that I should suggest calling her that, the name of one of the brightest stars in my feline galaxy; because I didn't even really like her that much at first sight!

Max and Ruth, my twin son and daughter, then about fifteen, had gone round to the people on the neighbouring property to select- a kitten from the litter they were trying to find homes for. The idea of getting another kitten at this juncture was to provide a companion and playmate for Lucy, the pretty little tabby-and-white stray who had recently joined the family, on the premise that two kittens were less, not more, trouble than one - usually a true assumption, for two kittens will play together then curl up and sleep together.

Exactly the reverse applies to puppies: two puppies can be relied upon to get into just about four times as much mischief as a single pup.

Anyway, to cut a long story short, Max and Ruth had selected Tabitha from a litter of five kittens; to be precise, they had chosen her out of the four female kittens in the litter, the solitary male being already spoken for.

When I looked at the odd grey kitten with the wild eyes, bat-like ears, stringy tail, gangly limbs and strange mottled grey coat that they proudly presented to me, I wondered what on earth the others could have been like if this, presumably, was the most prepossessing of the quartet. As they described to me, at great length, the special qualities of each kitten, I wondered still more.

'What shall we call her?' asked Max. 'Tabitha?', I suggested, and was amazed to hear myself: this Plain Jane bore not the slightest resemblance to my lovely long-gone Tabitha.

'Yes', the children agreed, 'We've never had a Tabitha'.

Now she had a name she 'belonged'. They put her down to explore her new domain. 'twenty seconds later, when she had shinned up the lounge-room curtains and was hurling the finest spate of invective (in, I presumed, Siamese) I had ever heard at the canine members of the family, I began to think that, ugly or not, she had possibilities!

Now, some years later, I wonder how I ever thought her plain. She has grown into her ears, her gangly limbs are now the epitome of sensuous grace, her - mottled grey coat I now describe as 'marbled blue' and her tail is no longer stringy 'two things have not changed: her command of 'Siamese' with its rich vocabulary and her contempt for dogs, though she soon learned not to retreat up curtains when she met them in the house. She came from a home where the dogs spent the greater part of their lives on chains. This she was brought up to consider right and proper: houses are for cats, and people. Kennels and chains for dogs.

As time went on, I found my affection for my ugly duckling growing deeper and stronger and also, somewhat to my surprise, that my naming of her had been curiously apt. Of all the cats I had loved and known down the years none resembled my first Tabitha so closely as this, the new Tabitha

Tabitha

- in character, in personality, even in her dislike and disdain for dogs; for it was a dog that came between the first Tabitha and me and caused us to part company.

I was then living at home with my parents, who had a beautiful Boxer bitch, Becky. Becky was invariably kind to the cats; in fact my little Tiny, when she was small, pink and hairless, used to walk over her outstretched body in front of the stove and settle down on the mat between her front and back legs, her bare back leaning against the big bitch's tummy.

However, for some reason I was never able to fathom, Tabitha took a dislike to Becky She began to actually lie in wait for her to come through doorways or round corners; then, furious and outraged, she would spring, yowling and spitting, for Becky's big domed head. At first the dog Would just shake her head violently in an attempt to work off this spitting fury with the needle-sharp claws that left crimson beads of blood where they sank in, but later her patience and tolerance grew understandably thin and she retaliated with fearsome growls and snarls.

It was painfully obvious that this state of affairs could not continue without one or the other getting seriously hurt. I knew that if Becky really lost her temper, and God knows Tabitha was giving her sufficient provocation, those strong jaws of hers were killers. I mentioned the problem to someone who had bought one of Tabitha's daughters and loved her dearly; she offered to give Tabitha a home if I would have her spayed.

I knew it was the only thing to do, and so, very sadly for me, I and the little cat who had given me so much happiness over the past few years came to the parting of the ways. She seemed, her new people said, delighted to meet her daughter again and settled happily into her new home.

So perhaps, if Tabitha is with me in a new body it is because, as the reincarnationists believe, she has a lesson to learn - namely how to live amicably with dogs. I wonder - often.

The ancient Egyptians and the Babylonians, who venerated the cat in their religious worship, believed that they had an important part to play: when a human who during his earthly life had attained a certain degree of holiness died, he needed a cat to guide him to paradise. This was done by the body of the cat acting as host to the soul of the dead person for the rest of its (the cat's) earthly life.

This belief has survived down the ages and even today there are Eastern people who believe that cats' bodies enshrine the spirits of the dead. Up until fairly recent times it was the practice when a member of the Royal House of Slam died to put a cat within the tomb of the departed. A small hole - an escape route - was always left for the cat, however. When ft emerged it was known that the soul had safely transmigrated and the cat was taken to the temple to be cared for with every luxury and attention for the rest of its earthly life.

As late as 1926, when the young King of Siam was crowned, a white cat was carried by the court chamberlain in the procession to the throne room. It was recognised that the old King would wish to be present at the coronation of his successor!

The belief that the bodies of cats enshrined the souls of the dead was not restricted to one point in time or one geographical place, but has been surprisingly widespread. Certain Gold Coast tribes believe that when people die their souls pass into cats, and in Japan black-and-white cats with a certain mark on their backs (said to represent a woman in a kimono) are called 'kimono cats'. It is believed by the members of certain sects that these cats house the souls of their ancestors and all such cats are sent to live in the temple.

One of the many strange paradoxes of the cat is that such a self-contained creature can arouse such strong emotions in people. As I have mentioned, few people are indifferent to cats: devotion or hatred are more usual reactions. The hatred often assumes an intensity that borders on the paranoid, and like most hatreds it has its roots in fear.

Even those of us who love cats may be touched with fear at times when we are at the receiving end of the cool, appraising stare that a cat can give. More than once I have been the victim of such a look from a pair of splendid feline eyes and have felt that my very soul was being looked over - and probably found wanting!

Sometimes too when we look into a cat's eyes it is almost as if we can see more than we expect to. I think Edward Carpenter must have experienced this when he wrote:

> *I saw deep in the eyes of the animals the human soul looking out upon me. I saw where it was born deep down under feathers and fur, or condemned for a while to roam four- footed among the brambles. I caught the clinging mute glance of the prisoner, and swore that I would be faithful.*

We may idly speculate *en passant* about our favourite cat's previous incarnations in human form, but I think most of us would really much rather believe that any other lives It has lived were in feline shape. Cats can sometimes be quite uncomfortable enough to live with as it is without the feeling that maybe we are sharing their lives and our home with, and are under constant scrutiny from, another human being who was probably greatly superior to us in every way!

Looking back over the many cats who have kept me company over the years there are many, divided in time, who are so alike that remembering them is sometimes more like remembering one cat than two.

First of all my deep cat friendships, dear old Muggins and, fifteen to twenty years later, Tilly - almost identical in both appearance and character. Beloved Tiny and Sheba who lives with me now. The two Tabithas - so alike in character and mannerisms that when I am woken in the wee hours by a furry figure wriggling under the bedclothes with me, or pushing her little cold nose into my face, or breaking into my dreams with a purr like a motorbike, the years seem to slide away and bemused by sleep I am not sure which Tabitha my hand reaches out to caress.

It is not, I am sure', coincidence that those I feel I may be meeting for the second time around, enjoying another of their fabled nine lives, are invariably those with whom I have had a particularly close relationship. Eva Gore-Booth in her book *The Inner Kingdom* said, 'Death is the absence of Love. Love brings us back to life, again and again, through reincarnations.'

The love that I am talking about here is a two-way thing, as much (or maybe more) on the part of the cat as the person involved. In fact only a great love on the part of the cat for someone still here on the earthly plane could warrant it ever wanting a return trip I feel. In fact the greatest argument against a possible return must be: why should they want to come back to a world and a people who often treat them shabbily?

Perhaps we who believe in reincarnation, both for ourselves and for our animal friends, are too ready to see in our new feline friends the spirit of one that has moved on? I think that sometimes we can be accused of this with justice. It is all too easy, with grief still tugging at our heartstrings, to choose a new kitten to resemble the old one and then to see in it qualities we remember in order - consciously or unconsciously - to mould it in a replica or reincarnation of our dead friend. We provide the same food, bed and dishes, slip into the same routine and habits, maybe even teach it the same tricks. This is easy to do but unfair - not only on our deluded selves, but on the kitten which we are not allowing to be an entity in its own right but forcing it to become a shadow of another self.

This is a very easy trap to fall into, but if we look on reincarnation as the instrument of karma, the great law of life which can very loosely be rendered by 'Whatever you sow, that you will also reap', we begin to see the taking on of another earthly life by a beloved cat as something more than a mere desire to share time with us once more. if we look on all forms of life as- steadily evolving and learning, then maybe we can see the lessons, and profit from them, as they come our way.

When she was a middle-aged to elderly cat, Muggins caught cat flu. It left her with a perpetual snuffle. When the vet suggested she be 'put down' because she was infecting all the younger cats and kittens and causing the repeated waves of cat flu that swept through our cat family, I acquiesced.

I can excuse myself now, with the wisdom of greater maturity and understanding of that other younger, harder me by saying that I was concerned to prove my practical good sense rather than my sensibility, and loath to admit that I owed a debt of love to a snuffly, elderly black-and-white moggy who had given me years of love and companionship. The look in her eyes as I handed her to the vet to take away still haunts me. I know now, and I knew then, though I would not admit it, that I had betrayed her - let her down. Apart from her snuffles she was in good health and life still had a sweetness for her to savour.

Perhaps with Tilly I was being given another chance; perhaps we both were. Isn't that the essential beauty of the whole doctrine of reincarnation. that we are all given the opportunity - over and over - to learn from our mistakes, to improve on our past record, to pay our debts? Many times I snatched Tilly from the jaws of death, cared for and nurtured her - without once thinking of euthanasia as a solution. The debt was paid when she died at the early age of eight and nothing I could do could save her: Muggins I had sent prematurely to her death, Tilly was taken from me barely hallway through what should have been her allotted span.

l am now very reluctant indeed to make that terrible decision to terminate a life and hope that in the future I shall make it only at the dictates of compassion rather than 'common sense'.

To those who scoff at the idea of our feline friends reincarnating in any form I can only pose the eternal question, 'Why not?'. It is impossible to live closely with a cat without being aware that 'something' very individual is housed within that small body. Why not spirit; and spirit, to quote Violet Tweedale, 'may be thought of as the nucleus of the reincarnating ego'.

To speak of the spirituality of animals is thought by many 'religious' people to be blasphemous for they contend that only man has the capacity for spirituality. But what is the definition of spirituality?

I have yet to find a better one than the words of 'Seth' as written by Jane Roberts in Seth Speaks:

> *Thus Spirituality is a thing of joy and of the earth, and has nothing to do with fake adult dignity. It has nothing to do with long words and sorrowful faces. It has to do with the dance of consciousness that is within you.*

Take this as the meaning of true spirituality and anyone will agree. that animals have as much, or more, spirituality than we humans. And among all the animals, cats with their sensuous pleasure in so many aspects of life and living, have their share. Certainly there can be few creatures more full of 'the dance of consciousness' than a playful kitten.

From the same source, the Seth material, we have some most interesting comments on reincarnation.

*Recently a great animal lover who is very aware
spiritually, in terms of 'New Age' thinking, put to me the
possibility that humans who have left this life may choose
to reincarnate as an animal in order to continue living in
close proximity to someone dearly loved and still living. It
is an idea that most people would quickly repudiate
because we are so certain that we are the superior
creatures. We can accept the promotion of an animal's
soul into a human body far easier than what we think of
as the demotion of a human's soul into an animal's body.
This is probably because we have far too simplistic an
idea both of time (which may not be progressive -
'vertical' - at all but static or 'horizontal') and of
reincarnation.*

Most people who believe in reincarnation, or even consider it
at all, do so in terms of a very simple concept of karma: 'Be
good in this life and you will come back into a better life: if you
are bad you will pay for it next time around.'

We also tend to see the soul as a neat, unsplittable package.
Perhaps we should be prepared to consider that the soul, or
the consciousness, which is probably a better word, need not
necessarily be confined to one body. In other words, soul,
consciousness, spirituality, psychic energy, whatever you like
to call it, can be portioned out.

Seth's explanation for this would seem to confirm the idea that
people can still be with us in the form of beloved animal
friends:

There is nothing to prevent a personality from investing a
portion of his own energy into an animal form. This is not
transmigration of souls. It does not mean that a man can be
reincarnated in an animal. It does mean that personalities can
send a portion of their energy into various kinds of form ... A
man is not an animal, then, nor does he invade the body of one.
He simply adds some of his energy to that present in the

animal, mixing this vitality with the animal's own. This does not mean that all animals are fragments in this manner however. Dogs, and other animals, are not simply the manifestation of stray psychic energy on the part of human beings.

Seth goes on to throw more light on the subject of animal consciousness, or, as we think of it, the animal soul, by saying:

> *Animals have varying degrees of self-consciousness, as indeed people do. The consciousness that is within them is as valid and eternal as your own. The mechanics of consciousness are the same. They do not change for animals or men. A dog is not limited to being a dog in other existences.*

If we can accept this, and certainly I find no difficulty in doing so, then my friend is correct in believing that there is something in our beloved animals of those we have also loved in human form. Maybe the little quirks and oddities of character that come through in our feline friends are some residue or fragment of their human personality? My Sheba has a most extraordinary passion for chocolate. However fast asleep she may appear, the smell of chocolate always wakes her and she will instantly demand it with a most annoying persistence, jumping on laps and reaching out a large white paw, claws extended, to grab a morsel of chocolate en route from human hand to mouth!

And so back to our nine lives: nine chances to cheat death, or nine return trips - or a bit of both? Maybe our little Hindu boy wasn't so wrong after all, and even in European cultures our cats can return?

Chapter 7
The Calculating Cat

Cats, I discovered very early on in my close acquaintance with them, are no fools: they weigh us mere mortals up very carefully and, having done so, they proceed to manipulate us. But even I was amazed when I received a letter from the new owners of one of the first Tabitha's daughters. Shot Silk, the blue tabby with the hazy red blurs, had proved to be an even more frivolous and abysmal mother than Tabitha, and I had decided that it would be less wearing on my nerves and probably a lot better for her if she were spayed and I found her a good home. I certainly succeeded in the latter.

I sold her to two charming ladies living in a delightful country house in Gloucestershire with one dog. Silky, I was quite sure, would be able to handle one dog. In the event she proved an adept at handling her new owners as well.

Brought up as she had been in a large family of kittens - not only her brothers and sisters, but Tiny's kittens as well - she had learned from an early age that when food appeared, you ate, and you ate quickly. She was also by nature a greedy cat, or so I had always thought, and would eat 'anything'. When her new owners had asked about her diet, I had told them this. Imagine my surprise when I got a worried letter a couple of weeks after her arrival.

Silky had settled perfectly in her new home and was no trouble at all with the dog. The only thing was her food. She resolutely refused to eat anything but the very best steak or white fish. Since I had told them she was on the greedy side and would eat anything the ladies were rather worried in case she was sick or fretting.

I was pretty sure she was neither. She had just summed up the situation, and her new owners, and decided that now she was 'only cat' with two obedient and doting slaves she was going to say how things should be done and just what her menu should be.

I wrote back and said I thought she was perfectly all right-just deciding to begin as she meant to go on. I suggested that they tried not to pander to her too much or she might become insufferable in her demands! The letter I had back assured me that they didn't mind at all buying her what she liked; they were just concerned that maybe she wasn't well, even though she seemed very happy and content, and to have settled well. They added the rather unnecessary piece of information that they absolutely adored her.

I often marvelled at how quickly this cat had summed up her new people and acted accordingly. Silky was probably no different from any other cat; she was just a little more blatant about It!

As a child I lived in a large English farmhouse. The kitchen window looked onto the garden, and of course into the kitchen. It had a wide stone sill where the cats loved to sit. It was also one of the cats' favourite 'doorways', providing a short cut to the back yard - through the kitchen and out of the back door, a very much shorter route than going round outside the house.

One never knew, when a cat pleaded eloquently at the window to be admitted, whether it really wanted to come into the kitchen or whether you were merely being used as a door opener to provide a short cut from the garden to the yard. Sometimes when I had done this umpteen times in one day, I felt righteously indignant at being used so by my feline friends.

We cat lovers are such suckers that it sometimes seems that the more calculating they are, the more we adore them. One of the most beloved members of my present cat family is Sheba, who is quite as calculating as they come.

I provided a bean bag by my bed specially for her. For some time she slept in it happily until one day it dawned on her that maybe my bed was better. From that moment on she has never slept in the bean bag. Instead she settles herself down in what she considers the best spot on the bed and there she stays.

I remember the first night she decided to change bean bag for bed. I came into the room to find John comfortably settled in his side of the bed and Sheba curled up in the middle of my half. When she saw me she uncurled slightly and looked at me with a look that said plainer than words, 'You can have the bean bag, I'm staying here!' and curled up tighter than ever In a gesture of utter dismissal. I didn't sleep in the bean bag, just for the record, but neither did Sheba. We all three came to a more or less amicable agreement about sharing the bed.

Sheba is utterly imperious. She demands things and attention, and goes into high dudgeon if her demands are not met immediately, or sooner. 'If you don't let me in at once,' she will say, 'then I shall go off for several days - and you know how that worries you!'

She has been known to go off for as long as four days at a time, living her secret cat life and returning when the family has just about given her up and gone into mourning for her. No doubt she finds the rapturous welcome that her belated return brings about very satisfying to her cat ego. When the door is opened for her she never stops to give polite thanks to the opener but sails past in an arrogant cloud of white fluff.

Fluffy on the other hand, though equally calculating when the mood takes her, is unfailingly polite when doors are opened for her and never fails to give a 'prrt!' of thanks, albeit graciously, to the humble opener.

Sheba

Probably one of the biggest delusions we humans hold about the cats in our lives and our relationship 'with them is in believing that we own them. Of all domestic animals the cat, surely, is the most free. Short of keeping it a prisoner twenty-four hours a day, who can force a cat to continue living with them if it decides it would rather leave?

One of the first kittens that Muggins ever had was Tilly, a tabby-and-white male; we mistook his sex at birth and thus misnamed him. Perhaps it was this initial insult that was instrumental in causing him to find another home!

This Tilly was a very affectionate and lovable cat, somewhat trying at times as a result of his extraordinary taste in food. He had a passion for tomatoes, raw, and if he happened to be in a room with a bowl of salad on the table, he would ignore any delicacies normally relished by cats, such as sliced hard-boiled egg, and eat all the tomatoes off the top.

He also had an absolute passion for dried fruit and would manage, somehow or other, to get into any cupboard, or climb onto the highest shelf and help himself (he could chew through or open any bag or carton) to my mother's carefully hoarded stores of raisins and sultanas. As this was in the immediate postwar days when such luxuries were rationed, this indulgence was by way of being a major crime.

For all that. we loved him dearly and made a great pet of him. We were very upset when he disappeared for a week and delighted to see him home again looking none the worse. A few weeks later he went again. Gradually his absences became longer and his stays at home shorter.

Soon they were about equal, and then he was away six weeks after a period at home of only a month. He always looked quite fit and happy when he returned, but inevitably the day came when he did not come back. We hoped that he had finally decided that his other home was the better of the two, not that something had happened to him. We could not help wondering why we had been found wanting. Maybe our appalling choice of a name had something to do with it!

Naming a cat is of course a very important thing. (It has been said that the true test of literary genius is whether or not one can name a kitten.) It is so important in fact that T.S. Elliot wrote a whole poem on the subject explaining that every cat must have at least three names, one sensible, one peculiar, and one known only to himself and the gods:

> *And that is the name that you never will guess:*
> *The name that no human research can discover -*
> *BUT THE CAT HIMSELF KNOWS, and will never*
> *confess.*

Is this a reminder of the old legend that every living creature, man and beast, has its own secret name and that anyone who learns the secret name of another gains complete sovereignty over him? I doubt if anyone has ever stumbled on a cat's secret name, for surely no living creature more jealously guards her own secret life than the cat.

Of all the animals, the domestic cat is probably about the only one that has managed to strike up a more or less equitable bargain with man. We keep cats for one of two reasons, generally speaking: for a utilitarian purpose, to keep down vermin, and for companionship. Both jobs they do extremely well - on their own terms and when they want to.

You can't take a cat out on a leash and say, 'Now - catch that mouse!' Or to be more precise, you can say it if you like but the chances of getting an obedient response are something like a thousand to one against. Neither can you command companionship.

There is of course a third reason for keeping cats. Medical research and experimentation. Here the cat it would seem has lost out entirely on the bargain. I would suggest that so has man, for he has lost even more than the cat - his integrity.

The cat, I think, has made an honest bargain with man, and keeps to it. Calculating the cat may be - but she is also completely straight about it. Cats just do not pretend; it is not their nature to feign a devotion they do not feel.

If Puss says she is pleased to see you when you come home, then she is pleased to see you. Of course it may only be because it is dinner time, but even then she will let you know quite plainly that is why she is pleased to see you.

It is not strictly true to say that cats cannot be persuaded to do things on command, or request. The ancient Egyptians after all did train their cats to go water fowling with them, taking them on leashes and sending them into the water to retrieve the birds they shot with bow and arrow.

Occasionally one gets a cat that will hunt with you, but the majority of cats, however good a mouser they may be, will resolutely refuse to cooperate if you seek their assistance in running down that mouse in the larder or lurking among the grain bags in the feed store.

Now and then, however, one will. Sox was one such. A big tabby son of Tilly, the much-travelled cat, he got his name because he wore sparkling white socks on all four feet.

Sox was such a cooperative fellow: standing by, watching and tensed to pounce, as you cautiously moved sacks of feed - and such a friendly, amiable soul in other ways that we turned a blind eye when a tiny chicken mysteriously disappeared and a small pile of wing feathers, incriminating evidence, were found in his favourite sun-baking spot! His greatest achievement was probably the day he caught three mice - at once. Poor fellow, he was really in a dilemma, with one under each front paw and one in his mouth: how could he deal with them without losing one?

The fact that Sox was unusual in his willingness to mouse with people proves that cats, on the whole, are more likely to be calculating than cooperative. The cat will keep your home free from vermin - sure she will; but because that is what she enjoys doing, not because you tell her to. She would still expect her bed and board whether or not she lifted a paw for you.

While no one can deny that the cat, when she wants to be, is among the best of companions (restful, soothing, even at times totally undemanding at others real company, even conversational company), it must also be admitted that it Is only when she wants to.

She is just as likely to be off somewhere about her secret cat business when you most need her, demanding your attention when you can least spare the time. But it is probably when looking after her creature comforts that the calculating side of the cat really comes to the fore. Anyone who has ever been foolish enough to admit a cat to the bedroom will soon discover that! Not only will she be sure she gets the warmest and most comfortable part of the bed, but at times it seems she will actually resent you sleeping in your own bed at all!

Tiny, who was always rather a 'touch-me-not' sort of cat. cherishing her own personal space, was a good bedroom companion because she always slept in her own bed, just by mine. Or almost always. One bitterly cold midwinter night I woke to find she had left her bed and wriggled into mine. She was lying against my thigh with her head the same way up as mine, purring softly. I didn't mind this at all, but I had little sleep for the remainder of the night because every time I moved the purring changed to a menacing growl and at least five, sometimes ten, needle sharp claws unsheathed and pressed into my skin.

Fluffy, my daughter's grey-and-biscuit-coloured fluffy cat, has the most flashingest eyes I have ever seen, and she~uses them to excellent effect. When she wants to sit in the armchair that you are already occupying. she simply sits on the arm, stares at you and flashes her eyes at you. when she does this I find it quite impossible to concentrate on my book, even though I am the sort of avid reader that can get quite lost in the printed word. Feeling. if possible, almost more annoyed with myself than with Fluffy, I have more than once moved to another chair whereupon she promptly settles herself in the one I have vacated!

Fluffy also uses her eyes to good effect when her favourite delicacies are on the menu. She has rather odd tastes, being passionately fond of broad beans and sweetcorn. She quite often uses her very sharp claws to underline the message of her flashing eyes, reaching up and inserting them swiftly and sharply into the seated posterior of her chosen victim.

Fluffy

Mother cats can also show a remarkable degree of shrewd thought when planning for their kittens' futures, or maybe when planning to shed the cares of motherhood.

When I was in my late teens we had a pretty little black-and-white cat, black with white shirt front and white paws. Silky was ostensibly an outdoor farm cat, who invariably had her kittens and kept them hidden from us till they were about weaning age. She would then hand over a family of wild little spitfires to us and, figuratively speaking, wash her hands of them.

On one occasion she really excelled herself. My father was working in his office when he was disturbed by a rustling in one of the cupboards among his papers. He stopped working and listened, but did not look. The cupboard was a built-in one in the corner of the room, and the house was old. He assumed that mice were among his papers, left his desk and went in search of a cat to deal with the intruders. The first cat he met was Silky He picked her up and carried her back to his office; bending down with the cat in his arms he cautiously opened the cupboard door.

What he saw was not mice, or even a mouse, but three black-and-white kittens staring at this monster intruder in their safe hidey-hole with startled eyes, bristling fur and prickling whiskers, three little mouths opened in unison displaying bright pink little tongues as they spat at him.

As for Silky, her expression quite plainly said, 'Well, I don't know what you've brought me here for; but now you've found them they're your responsibility!' And she turned round and stalked out of the office. My father shut the cupboard door and followed her. He fetched me to help deal with the situation, Silky having made it abundantly plain that as far as she was concerned, the kittens were reared.

They were little viragos, equipped with at least twice the normal complement of teeth and claws, it seemed. They had been hidden so well for the first six weeks of their lives (they had never seen a human being, at close range anyway) that we needed leather gloves to handle them Even then we were at something of a loss what to do with them. As my mother happened to be out at the time and not there to stop us, we did what seemed the easiest thing at the time. We simply took them across the hall to the least-used room in the house, the drawing room. Unfortunately we had forgotten that it was summer and there was an empty hearth. Two of the kittens shot under furniture and spat at us, while the third, the fieriest of the lot, shot up the chimney and disappeared from sight. Down into the hearth and across the hearthrug onto the carpet came a cloud of black soot.

After several futile attempts to get him down, even to see him, my father stayed in the room to stop the other two going after h~m, and I went in search of Silky once more. It took me some time to find her this time, but when I did she obligingly called her recalcitrant child down; he came, together with another load of soot and my father grabbed him, forgetting that he had discarded the leather gloves, and got his finger bitten through almost to the bone for his pains. Silky gave us a withering look which conveyed pretty plainly that she really thought us hopeless kitten minders and that this was the last time she would come to our rescue, and stalked off.

We blocked up the chimney and cleared up the mess. Incredibly, in the space of a week, two of the kittens were quite tame. It took a little longer with the chimney sweep, but by the time they were eight weeks old we had them all sufficiently tame and civilised to go out into the world to new homes.

Silky's behaviour, I always felt, was a supreme example of the calculating ability of cats. what is more, she is not the only cat I have known behave just like that. Many years later, when living in Australia, we moved over to Victoria from Tasmania with our family of neutered cats, to find a semi-tame tortoiseshell female left in the house we had bought, together with two of her offspring. We called her Mummy Puss, and were fortunate enough to find homes for those two kittens. But of course she had more ...

I kept one kitten of the next litter, a rich red Tabby male. By dint of being as calculating as any cat I had both won her confidence and managed to shut her up in a shed with a cosy bed in it to have the kittens, so I was able to remove the others and humanely destroy them at birth, deeming this ultimately more humane action than leaving her to rear a whole litter with no certainty of homes for them.

When the kitten was just opening its eyes I made the mistake of showing him proudly to my husband, and the even worse mistake of letting Mummy Puss see that he had seen the kitten. I knew it was a mistake the minute I had done it and saw the way she looked at John.

That night the kitten was missing. Mummy Puss was there for her tea, but there was no sign of the kitten. I knew that she had hidden it away for safety. But where? Careful watching convinced me that he was hidden somewhere in the thick bushes on the other side of the creek.

Shortly after this we had torrential rain and flash floods. We were marooned on our side of the creek. We didn't see Mummy Puss so I presumed she was marooned on her side. I looked at the brown waters of the swollen creek swirling up the banks and lapping round the blackberry bushes. where was the kitten?

Nearly ten days later when the waters subsided, Mummy Puss reappeared for her meals. I had more or less given up the kitten for lost, no doubt washed out of his hidey-hole and drowned. But about six weeks after he was born, Mummy Puss brought him to the house, put him in a carefully selected 'safe' place under the house round the back - and that was it. He was now our responsibility. She had done her bit, rearing him and nurturing him through the floods; now we could take over.

Unfortunately, as she had also kept him safe from people, including us, what she had reared and was handing over to us was a wildcat. But alas, a wildcat still far too young to fend for himself.

The fates that look after small kittens were attentive, however. Ruth, my daughter, then eight years old, was not only a passionate cat lover, but imbued with endless patience and, this being school holidays, endless time. Hour after hour she sat outside his sanctuary under the house talking to him and coaxing him out with food and milk. Finally she could actually hold him. I well remember the first time she brought him into the house: although he had become tolerably bold by now he panicked totally inside the house and both Ruth and I were covered in long red scratches as we endeavoured to calm him down and prevent him escaping into some other inaccessible hideout.

We called him Wilbur and he grew into an exceptionally handsome cat, a deep, deep red Tabby with a sleek and glossy coat, not a ginger but a true marmalade cat. Surprisingly, once he finally accepted us as friends, he also became a sensible, level-headed and calm cat who took two moves to different houses with us in his stride.

Perhaps old Mummy Puss's calculating went even further than we imagined. By presenting him to us and then totally ignoring him (as far as I could see, she never went near him, to feed or wash him or anything), she forced us to take charge, to adopt him as our own, and that ensured his future.

Cats are such deep, mysterious creatures, their lives so dichotomised into the life we are privileged to see and their intensely private secret life that it is hard to make any judgements of any sort about their characters or their motives - which does not of course stop us, - as humans, doing just that!

Chapter 8
The Cat Possessed:
Witches and Cats

Most of us, when we think of witches, imagine an old crone soaring skywards aboard her broomstick, perched behind her a smug, satanic black cat. That is the witch of the fairy story What of the reality?

To find out how the cat first became involved with the cult of witchcraft it is necessary to go back to Ancient Egypt. The gods of the Ancient Egyptians were neither man nor beast, but a blend of the two, usually depicted as humans with animal heads. Supreme among these deities was the great goddess Pasht (some people think the name Puss is a derivative of this), the cat-headed goddess. Pasht was considered the beloved companion of the great Ra, the sun-god, himself, and as such she became identified with the female aspects of the god, particularly Isis, the moon goddess.

Witches were once the priestesses of the great moon goddess, Isis, Diana or Luna, known as the Queen of Heaven, the Great Mother of all life. So we can see that the link between witches and cats goes back far beyond the nursery tales of our childhood into antiquity.

The Egyptians connected the cat with the moon, and witches were believed to get their powers from the moon which in itself was held to hold enormous sway over all life. We know how the moon affects the tides; ancient alchemists taught that almost all forms of life were affected by the waxing and waning phases of the moon, from the weight of men's bodies to the sap circulating in the trees. To ensure success therefore, it was necessary to plant crops, fell trees, extract juice from grapes, etc., at the correct time. The moon also was the planet that controlled the brains of men: the beliefs (still held by some) that the mentally disturbed become more violent with the full moon, or that other- wise normal people can suffer from moon madness, can be traced way back into antiquity and has given us words such as lunatic and lunacy.

Down the ages witches were credited with the power of controlling all these remarkable forces of the moon - even, in the case of some, of controlling the moon herself. As Shakespeare says in The Tempest, A witch: and one so strong, she could control the moon ...it is not hard to see why witches found the cat an invaluable ally. Linked as she was to the moon who herself controlled the elements, it is no wonder that the cat's help was sought by medieval witches when they wished to raise a storm! Even today we can find many relics of this belief. It is popularly believed in many parts of the world that a cat frolicking unduly foretells a gale, and the light breeze that ripples the surface of the water before a squall is often referred to by sailors as a 'cat's paw'.

Witches, trading on the belief that cats, and thus they, could raise winds at will, 'sold' favourable winds to the sailors throughout the fifteenth, sixteenth and seventeenth centuries. This was a practice, however, which could prove as dangerous as it was profitable, for there are many cases solemnly recorded in the annals of British law courts that accuse witches of causing the loss of ships at sea through storms.

The worship of sacred animals began in Egypt before the dawn of history. Not only the cat but the ram, the bull and the hawk were represented by gods. But the cat had special qualities and the Egyptians placed great faith in her powers of protection, both in this life and the next. Those who were not fortunate enough to possess a living cat had small statues or charms of cats. These were often buried with a person to help the soul on its perilous journey through the Nether world to paradise. We can see a residue of this belief lingering on today in the 'lucky black cat' charms and emblems.

Much nearer to home in time and place than the cat worship of Ancient Egyptians or even the medieval witches of Europe and their cats, is Rosaleen Norton, the well-known Sydney artist.

Her paintings, as well as her love of cats, linked her with the culture of Ancient Egypt, for many were of supernatural deities which she depicted as a fusion of animal and human. They were a fusion of the two, rather than a straightforward half-animal, half-human god. For example, she made Jupiter a proud potentate with a majestic beard, leonine legs and a tail and with a light emanating from his forehead. Her painting of Mars with the winged head of a~hawk, scorpion's tail, clawed feet and powerful male human torso gives a great sense of aggressive strength.

She lived in a basement flat in an ageing block near the famous El Alamein fountain in Kings Cross, Sydney, becoming known as 'The Witch at Kings Cross'. She virtually became a recluse for the last few years of her life, avoiding people and expressing a belief in the superiority of cats, who, she felt, embodied the spiritual sensitivity lacking in mankind as a whole. She died in Sydney in December 1979.

In their book *Other Temples, Other Gods: A Study of the Occult in Australia*, Neville Drury and Gregory Tillet wrote of her:

Rosaleen Norton felt that the animal kingdom had retained its integrity to a far greater extent than the human. She was at one with the animals, for whom she felt a natural empathy. Many human beings, however, she despised for their narrow world view. Cats, by contrast, operate in the waking consciousness and on the astral plane simultaneously.

Wiccan, witchcraft or what is often simply called 'The Old Religion' is not, as many suppose, something confined to fairy tales, folklore or our pagan past. It is a tradition that is very much alive in the world today. The increased interest in witchcraft is probably explained by the fact that it is seen by many people as a nature religion, and as we all know, there is a vigorous 'back to the earth' movement throughout the world.

Witches have always had animals around them, both in the past and today (in fact during the terrible years of the medieval witch hunts if a lonely old woman kept a cat for company it was often enough to start the whispers and rumours that would lead her to the stake). Today, as Clair and Simon Lorde, two present-day Australian witches, told me:

> *Wiccans have not changed their attitude to animals: it remains as it ever was. You would not find a witch's household bare of creatures. We use them as familiars. We do become quite furious when we read of mutilations, and the usual rot that 'witches may have done it'. Nothing could be further from the truth!*

What exactly is a familiar? The dictionary defines it as a supernatural spirit often assuming animal form, supposed to attend and aid a witch, wizard, etc.

Witches enjoy the company of all animals and may choose any as a familiar, but cats are more often associated with them than any other animals. No doubt this again traces back to Egypt when cats were credited with special occult powers and revered as gods. The Ancient Celts believed that the eyes of a cat were windows through which humans could explore the inner world.

The following instructions for the occult training of a cat are taken from a Book of Shadows of long ago.

*To be performed every evening, at the same time, in the
same place. Take your cat to sit close by you. Face it in the
same direction you face, which should be the glorious
place of moonrlse. Firmly, but gently, expressing love
through your hands, stroke your friend until your breath
and its purring breath become one. Both your friend and
yourself will now possess the same matters of will, your
eyes and his will see all, and travel together. The power of
all spells and enchantments will now be doubled, nay
tripled, through the loving care of your familiar!*

Perhaps these instructions explain more clearly the actual role
of a familiar as a sort of psychic battery boosting the occult
powers of the witch herself! Mediums who like their animals
with them during seances are using their spiritual qualities in
much the same way.

Simon and Clair Lorde give instructions for actually choosing a
pet as a familiar. Do not, they say, go for any particular breed,
colour or sex, but 'seek an inwardly sensed mystic quality and,
rather than choosing an animal, let it choose you!'

'Having chosen it, the naming is all-important. Do not be in a
hurry; but try out several names, finally selecting one that
somehow seems to "fit" best and evokes the most response in
the one being named.'

On the subject of familiars, I have a great admiration for the
witches of old, for I find it extraordinarily hard to breathe in
time with either Sheba's or Tabitha's purring, these two being
my closest cat friends. So difficult in fact that the thought has
crossed my mind that they are making it difficult: that
perhaps they prefer being their own very secret selves and do
not want me sharing the all-seeing all-knowing psychic places
within them?

Stories of women using cats as familiars and donning their
bodies at will are legion in the annals of witchcraft trials.

Though it may seem incredible that people were tried for their lives and condemned on such evidence, not one but literally thousands of so-called witches were put to death on the testimony of their neighbours that they turned themselves into cats. A typical case was that of the Witches of Aberdeen, who in 1596 were accused of turning themselves into cats to celebrate their orgies around Fish Cross. This was the scene of a fish market, and the so-called witches were probably nothing more than a group of harmless, hungry cats, drawn there by the smell of their favourite food.

In 1607 Isobel Grierson was convicted of witchcraft and burnt. The evidence against her? That she went into the house of one Adam Clark and his wife at night in the likeness of his own cat, accompanied by a great rabble of cats. According to the story the cats were accompanied by the devil in the form of a black man who seized the poor maid of the household by the hair. Corroborating evidence was brought by Mr Brown in the same town who also claimed that she visited him at night in the shape of a cat.

At the trial for witchcraft of Janet Irving in 1616 we have a twist to the usual woman-in- the-form-of-cat evidence when it was said that the devil, when in the form of a woman, changed into a cat and ran away when he heard the name of Christ spoken.

That such testimony could be offered, accepted and the accused actually forfeit their lives on it almost defies belief, yet the records of such cases would fill many volumes.

Witches - that is, real witches, followers of the old religion - probably helped to give rise to such incredible beliefs by their habit of wearing masks and furs when meeting for their sacred rituals. Also, because they often took drugs with a hallucinatory effect, many witches actually believed that they did change into animal form.

Witchcraft is really the survival (perhaps with the resurgence of such beliefs today we should say revival) of the worship of the feminine principle in God. Christianity, which superseded the Old Religion in Europe, had a masculine deity in direct contrast to all the old beliefs which had seen the creator always as the eternal mother.

No doubt the many superstitions that abound about cats are relics of the days when cats held such an important place in the world of the occult. It is universally accepted that pure black cats are lucky, and the reverse is often held of white cats - so much so that some people will refuse to give house room to a pure white cat. A cat with extra toes is considered especially lucky and in the north of England a Tortoiseshell cat is considered to be the best possible insurance against fire.

There are countless stories too, in the records of British Law, of cats causing storms at sea. One of the most famous of Scottish witches was Agnes Sampson, who was accused of trying to shipwreck King James on his journey home from Denmark. At first she vehemently denied this but after torture 'confessed' to having, in the company of other witches, christened a cat, then bound it to parts of a dead man, and thrown it into the sea, after which 'there did arise such a tempest in the sea as a greater hath not been seen'. She further admitted that the king only got home safely because his faith had been stronger than her witchcraft.

In Europe Charlemagne decreed the death penalty for those who, by means of the devil, disturbed the air and excited tempests. And in 1484 Pope Innocent VIII explicitly charged sorcerers with these practices.

Cats are extremely sensitive to atmosphere and changes in the weather, but this of course does not mean that they actually cause them. There is an old Slavic belief that in thunderstorms cat's bodies are inhabited by devils and that it is wise to clear cats out of the house in a thunderstorm because in order to drive the devils out of the cats, the angels send dawn shafts of lightning which are liable to set the house on fire! In Ireland cats were often seized and kept captive in metal pots during storms until they used their special powers to bring about calm weather!

We have all heard the superstition that when a cat washes behind her ears, it foretells rain; in Scotland a cat rubbing against a table leg is said to bring gales. but few of us today believe that they are any more responsible for bad weather than the TV weather men who predict it!

It is not really surprising that cats should be linked with the occult and to mysterious. Surely the whole essence of the cats' fascination is that she is unfathomable. No other creature can move so silently or blend in so completely with its surroundings. Who can see a black cat sitting in the darkest places on a dark night? Or a black-and-silver striped tabby moving through silver-striped shadows made by a full moon shining through the branches of trees!

What could be more spine-chilling than the gleam of real live cats' eyes glinting green as the light catches them? Only the similar glint of Siamese cats' blue eyes glowing red under similar conditions. Such a sight can be so awe-inspiring that a friend of mine with two Siamese told me her Spanish cleaning lady crossed herself every time this happened!

If this could evoke such a superstitious response in the latter half of the twentieth century, then how much more so must it have done in less enlightened ages?

I can remember returning late at night after a theatre outing to be greeted by Paddy, my ginger neutered tom. As I stepped out of the car and bent down to stroke him, his fur crackled and the sparks literally flew, clearly visible in the darkness. One can readily imagine what awe this sort of thing would have created in medieval minds!

And what of white cats with odd eyes? When the artificial light caught my beloved little Tiny's eyes, one would glow red and the other flash the normal fluorescent green.

Yes, it is easy to see how the most innocent and innocuous of household cats could become something much more sinister: the cat possessed - and possessing - of witches and witchcraft. And, if we are truthful, isn't that a great deal of her attraction for us - the possibility that our own cat may not, after all, be quite what she appears to be?

Chapter 9
Cats and Christianity

It will be noticed that cats are conspicuous by their absence in the canonical books of the Bible. This may be partially explained by the fact that the Jews, the Twelve tribes of Israel, were for the most part a wandering people. The cat, symbol of home and hearth, does not as a rule take kindly to a nomadic way of life. There are of course exceptions that prove the rule (two cats I know travel Australia quite happily with their owner who is a circus proprietor).

Another, more plausible reason is that the Jews had an almost fanatical hatred for everything connected with the Egyptians, for so long their rulers and taskmasters. The Egyptians venerated the cat as most sacred of all the sacred animals.

Animal lovers often find it hard to reconcile the Jesus of the gospels with a teaching that does not appear to take into consideration kindness to animals. In actual fact all Jesus' teachings emphasise the all-embracing love of the Creator for all life. The story of the five sparrows sold for two farthings is all too often told in such a way that it emphasises the greater importance of man than sparrow; the fact that sparrows too are important and that their death is a cause of sorrow, is glossed over.

Jesus, we remember, spent the most impressionable years of his childhood in Egypt. It seems inconceivable that, in those years, he did not come into close contact with cats! The fact that they are not mentioned in the gospels could well be due to the fact that those books were written by Jewish scribes.

This omission is-remedied by a remarkable volume called The Gospel of the Holy Twelve. The contents of this book were received in vision by the Rev. G.J. Ouseley. He also received the information that the work was a translation of an early Christian document preserved in a Buddhist monastery, where it had been hidden for safety by members of an Essene community. Since many of the early scriptures claim to have been delivered to their writers by means of visions then it seems quite logical to judge it more on its content than its means of delivery.

There are many stories of animals in this gospel. The story of the nativity; for instance, includes a cat and her kittens in the stable. Another story tells how as Jesus was passing through a village with his followers he saw a group of idlers tormenting a cat. Jesus tried to reason with them but they took no notice and merely abused him as well. He then made a whip of knotted cords and tried to drive them away, but the worst of them went on defying him. Jesus reached out his hand and the young man's arm withered. Next day his mother came and begged Jesus to restore the arm. Jesus did so, but first he spoke to them all of the law of love and the unity of all life, saying, 'As you do in this life to your fellow-creatures, so will it be done to you in the life to come.

On another occasion when Jesus was entering a village.

> *He saw a young cat which had none to care for her, and she was hungry and cried to him and he took her up, and put her inside his garment, and she lay in his bosom. And when he came into the village he set food and drink before the cat, and she ate and drank, and showed thanks to him. And he gave her to one of his disciples who was a widow, whose name was Lorenza, and she took care of her.*

(I have always found this a particularly charming little story, especially the bit about the cat showing her thanks. I can just

114

imagine the soft feline smile and the purr of thanks and contentment.) Some of his followers murmured among themselves at his 'oddity' in bothering about a stray cat, But hearing them he turned and told them:

These are your fellow-creatures of the great household of God; they are your brothers and sisters, having the same breath of life in the Eternal. Whosoever careth for one of these and gives it food and drink in its need, does it unto me. And whoever willingly suffers one to be in want and does not defend it when evilly treated suffers the evil to be done to me. For as you have done in this life so shall it be done to you in the life to come.

For the second Time we have Jesus teaching and warning in connection with a cat!

It may be even that such simple and homely little stories were in fact parts of the original gospels as we know them but were dropped as part of the deliberate 'playing down' of the cat by the early Church masters.

It is a matter of historical fact that as one religion supersedes another it must in some way negate or displace the gods of the vanquished faith. As Christianity spread and took over from the old pagan religions it became necessary to remove the great cat goddess from her pedestal. Thus we find the cat slipping into obscurity and the goddess herself, the great goddess of both chastity and fertility reappearing in a different guise - as the Virgin Mary.

In the Middle Ages we find the cat fallen indeed; she became the symbol of man's guilt for the crucifixion - a scapegoat. Many Italian paintings of the Last Supper show a cat, too often seated at the feet of the traitor Judas Iscariot for the significance of its position to be missed.

Cats were often made to bear the punishment for human sin. There is a case on record of a woman condemned for murder in France who was burned to death along with fourteen cats. One of the most blatant examples however was the custom of whipping a cat to death at Shrovetide, the beginning of Lent, the traditional time to confess sins. - This seemed to be particularly popular at Albrighton, a village not so far from my English birthplace, where an inn sign commemorated this practice with the couplet: 'The finest pastime that is under the sun, is whipping the cat at Albrighton.

By the fifteenth century, when the fear of witches became a mania and vindictiveness respectable, the massacre of thousands of women and cats was seen as a 'casting out of evil spirits'. At the coronation of the first Elizabeth a wickerwork dummy of the Pope was filled with live cats and thrown on a huge bonfire. Pious Protestants declared the cats' shrieks to be the 'language of the devils within the body of the Pope'. Later in the reign of Catholic Mary it was considered holy amusement to shave a cat's head, dress it up so that it represented a Puritan and hang it publicly.

Even as late as the middle of the nineteenth century it is recorded how, on the first Sunday in Lent, a cat was ritually burned at the stake in Picardy.

There were, however, some enlightened souls who did not see the cat as the representative of evil. She shared the fate of many witches, but she also found refuge among holy women within convent walls. In the British Museum there is a delightful sketch by Leonardo da Vinci for a painting of the Virgin and Child in which the Child is shown playing with a kitten.

Several artists included a cat in their paintings of the Holy Family. Most famous is probably Barocchio's 'Madonna Del Gatto' which hangs in the British National Gallery. The cat, which is sitting up in a begging position playing with the infant John the Baptist, is a delightful ginger-and-white. The Virgin is pointing the cat out to the baby Jesus while a smiling St Joseph looks on.

Art, and literature, particularly poetry, seem to be excellent guidelines down the ages to the status of the cat in society. There is a curious dearth of poetry on cats in the Western (Christian) world between the eighth century, when an anonymous Irish poet wrote about his cat Pangur,

> *More than fame I love to be*
> *Among my books and study;*
> *Pangur does not grudge me it,*
> *Content with his own merit.*

and the fourteenth century, when Chaucer wrote somewhat unflatteringly of the cat, comparing the Wife of Bath to her. However as the long night of the Dark Ages recedes to herald the dawn of the Renaissance we find a burgeoning of feline poetry, and we can assume that just as the cat was being reinstated in literature so she was in everyday life.

The attitude of the Christian Church towards animals has been both ambiguous and contradictory down the centuries. On the one hand we have Descartes, the Catholic philosopher, with his theory that animals were mere 'things', automatons without feeling.

This view was also held by Father Rickaby in his *Moral Theology*, published in 1888: 'Brutes are things in our regard and we are right in using them unsparingly.' *The Catholic Dictionary*, published in 1897, said much the same thing:

> *They are not created by God. They have no rights. The*
> *brutes are made for man, who has the same right over*
> *them which he has over plants and stones. He may kill*
> *them for his food ... put them to death or inflict pain on*
> *them, for any good or reasonable end, such as the*

117

promotion of man's knowledge, health, etc, or even for the purpose of recreation.

Happily there was such a storm of protest over the above paragraph that it was subsequently withdrawn. But the damage, it seemed, had been done. There are many people who genuinely believe that the Christian Church, particularly the Roman Catholic Church, does not admit the possibility that animals could have immortal souls, or even advocate kindness towards them. In actual fact Christian voices raised in support of animals are numerous, but alas, for the most part unheard or unheeded.

St Martin De Porres, the South American saint, not only established orphanages and hospitals but also ran what must have been one of the first known homes for cats and dogs. One of the best-known stories about Martin tells how he persuaded a dog, a rat, a cat and a bird to share the same dish in perfect harmony.

St Martin was born in Lima in 1579, the son of a Spanish knight and a Negro woman. At the age of fifteen he entered the Dominican order as a lay brother. He had such a rapport with animals that when the monastery was overrun by a plague of rats he persuaded them to leave by talking to them and promising to feed them if they would leave the monastery.

Many thinking people today see the practice of vivisection as the darkest shadow on the universal conscience of mankind. Thousands of cats annually are the victims of what many people believe to be a practice as sinister and evil as black magic.

The fact that for the most part, the Churches remain silent on this subject causes many people to turn away from them. But it has not always been so. In the Nineteenth century there was no louder or clearer voice speaking out against vivisection than the English Cardinal Manning. As Vice-President of the

British Anti-Vivisection Society he was a tireless and outspoken speaker.

'Between sanctioning its atrocities and stopping the practice altogether there is no middle course', he said unequivocally, in one of his speeches. 'By prohibiting vivisection you will at one and the same time save numberless animals from pangs which add no small item to the sum of misery on earth, and men from acquiring that hardness of heart and deadness of conscience for which the most brilliant discovery of physiology would be poor compensation.'

Alas, nearly a hundred years after his death vivisection is carried on in the Christian world on a scale undreamed of by His Eminence, the cardinal.

There seems to be a peculiar affinity between cardinals and cats! Cardinal Wolsey was renowned for his love of cats; his favourite one always sat with him, often asleep in the folds of his robe, when he held audience.

France's Cardinal Richelleu was a passionate cat lover. History records that with one hand he caressed the cat on his knee while with the other he signed an order for the execution of Cinq-Mars. At the time of his death he had fourteen cats and he left a pension for them to ensure that they were cared for.

Perhaps it is not just cardinals but clerics in general that attract cats, and the higher up the ecclesiastical scale the better, for many Popes have been renowned as lovers of our friend the cat.

Leo XII, Gregory X and Pius IX were all renowned for their love of cats. The latter had a cat who always dined with him, sitting on its own chair at the table. Nearer in time, in a biography of Pope Paul VI, who died in 1978, John G. Clancy tells of the only time he ever saw him really angry. Giovanni Battista (as the Pope then was) was only seven years old at the time. Another boy tied an old frying pan to a cat's tail, scaring it out of its wits. The future Pope was so angry that he went for the boy with fists flying.

When the present Pope was elected he had his cat flown to Rome from Poland. A delightful photo of the pontiff with his small friend in his arms appeared on the front cover of *The Ark* (April 1982).

The Ark is the quarterly magazine of the Catholic Study Circle For Animal Welfare which, in spite of its name, is quite an ecumenical movement and has branches in many parts of the world, including Australia. Many other Christian Churches such as the Anglican Church and the Society of Friends in England, have animal welfare societies, so we may hope that the Christian Church as a whole is gradually moving towards an acceptance of animals as the sensitive and sentient creatures so many people know them to be.

Chapter 10
Cats and Healing

In recent years there has been a great upsurge of interest in healing - that is, the use of one's personal energies to restore the wellbeing of another creature. A few years ago this was perhaps more commonly referred to as 'faith healing' or 'spiritual healing', but nowadays the simpler term 'healing' is often preferred. Healing has been described as a flow of energy from one person to another. Cats can both receive and give this flow and can thus be either healed or healers.

We have, perhaps because of the advances in medical science, come to look at healing as something done to us from outside. This is not strictly accurate, for true healing comes from within. Medical or any other treatment can only help the body regain health. And any doctor or surgeon will tell you that the patient's will to live is the most important factor for the successful outcome of any form of treatment or operation.

A veterinary practitioner I knew in England who had a very large city practice of small animals told me that in cats, more than any other creature, this will to live was most crucial. Without it, he told me, cats would die when there was no need for them to; with it they could survive almost anything.

Healing energy is not a gift given to the favoured few. it is something we all have. The healers are those who learn to tap it. Try this simple experiment. Place your two hands in front of you, fingertips up, in a classical 'praying' gesture. Do not let them touch but keep the palms a centimetre or so apart. Concentrate your attention on them, imagining, if it helps something between them - a piece of plasticine, a pliable ball,

Move your hands very slightly as if rolling it between them, but do not let them actually touch.

After a short while you will feel a slight warmth in your hands, followed by a tingling in the fingers. You may even get small red patches on the palms and the tingling may be so strong it feels like an electric shock - the same 'shock', in fact, that you can feel sometimes when you stroke your cat.

I was relaxing in an armchair one evening with Shea on my lap. She had one of her recurring bouts of eczema, something to which white cats, unfortunately, seem particularly prone. As she relaxed purring on my knee I was passing my hands, not quite close enough to be actually stroking, over the area, hoping to direct a flow of healing energy.

On one of my fingers I had a sticking plaster covering a small, but quite deep, cut I had inflicted on myself as I sliced vegetables with my mind on something else. I had done it a couple of days previously and this evening I noticed it was particularly 'angry' and that it was throbbing quite painfully.

As I passed my hand over Shea body the throbbing seemed to accentuate and the finger felt quite hot. When I had finished 'healing' her it subsided. I felt no more from it and next morning when I peeled off the plaster it was quite healed. Shea's eczema? Yes, that seemed better too!

We often give healing to our cats without being aware of doing so. Once when my first Tabitha was a half-grown cat she was suddenly and mysteriously very sick. What it was I will never know. I sat by her for most of the night as she lay in her bed, on her side, breathing strangely. I thought, with the intellectual part of me, that she was going to die. So did everyone else in the family I was determined, with the emotional part of me, that she wouldn't. As I sat by her I talked softly to her and stroked her. In the early hours of the morning she changed position and began to purr. Exhausted, I went to bed and slept. When I got up for breakfast she got out of bed and greeted me, her old self.

Probably the most crucial point when a dearly loved cat is very sick is our caring and our love which we impart to them and thus greatly strengthen their all-important will to live.

In the long weeks of Tiny's sickness I feel this is what helped her - but only helped her: her own indomitable spirit and determination to survive was what pulled her through. Similarly, when Tilly was hit by a car and left for dead at the roadside, it was her spirit that saved her; but the vet who treated her and left her at home instead of taking her back to his surgery knew that her spirit might well flag and wilt without the support of home and those she knew.

Nearer in time is Kit, the kitten in the pet shop who 'told' Ruth to buy her. Watching her get sicker and sicker, and actually shrink instead of grow, was like a re-enactment of the nightmare weeks of Tiny's terrible illness all those years ago. Twice it seemed as if she must die, or rather that she could not live. The tiny body was so frail, so dehydrated. Fortunately I now knew a little about the transfer of energy and the power of healing. I laid her on my lap and passed my hands over her body, willing strength and life into her. I was rewarded by a thin croaky purr. Kit lived, and today she is an exquisite little cat with huge round eyes which look at you with such intensity that you feel she can see your very thoughts.

Poor little Tiny: so much seemed to happen to her. When still a very young cat, before I had her spayed, she developed a large mammary cyst and had to go to the vet for surgery. It was so large that she had no less than four stitches to close the incision. It was with a heavy heart that I felt the lump recurring a year or so later.

I was, however, then writing some animal articles for a little magazine called Global Light. The editor of this magazine was

Gordon Turner, a spiritualist and a healer. I knew that he did absent healing and that he also healed animals. I asked him to put Tiny on his healing list. I didn't do it with any great faith, but in a 'We'll give it a go' and 'it can't do any harm anyway' frame of mind. The morning I got his letter back to say that healing had started, and would I tell him when (not if) the lump had gone, I noticed it was smaller. Within a week it disappeared altogether and she never had a recurrence.

Gordon Turner did not specialise, he treated animal and human alike, just as the herbalist of the past would treat man or beast, and the bone setter set broken bones whether the patient was two or four-legged. Gordon wrote in his book, *An Outline of Spiritual Healing*:

> *Healing power is not restricted to any one life form. The same healing that will ease the arthritis in the legs of a human patient will just as readily ease the pain of an animal. All life is part of the Supreme Spirit. There is not one healing for animals and another for people. We have the same God and we react to the same power of love. At one time he held separate clinics for animals and people. Deciding this was unnecessary he just held one clinic. He had no complaints from the human patients and found that the animals behaved perfectly and did not quarrel among themselves.*

Gordon found his animal patients so appreciative that it was sometimes difficult to get rid of them. A cat he had been treating once a week for a tumour turned up, on her own, for two successive weeks after she no longer needed treatment. Her owners only stopped her setting off across town, over busy streets, on these days by shutting her up!

He refers to the healing power as 'the energy of love' and in a delightful anecdote about a small black kitten he tells how he learned from it that this power is limitless.

He was called early one morning to treat a kitten that had been run over. Dressing hurriedly he went with the caller to a flat in North London. However, when they got there a vet had been called and had just given the kitten an injection to end its sufferings. It lay on the floor, a pathetic black scrap - dead.

'Obviously,' he wrote, 'there was nothing I could do, but seeing the owner's distress I suggested we kneel together with our hands above the kitten and pray for the easy passing of its spirit to a happier land.'

They had been kneeling like this for two or three minutes when 'I felt a strange sensation under my hands. It was just as if fur was being rubbed against the palms. I looked down and saw, to my amazement, that it had lifted itself to its feet and was rubbing its back against my hands'. The kitten then began to purr, walked across the room to its bowl, drank some milk and went on to live to maturity and normal cat life.

Marilyn Preston is an English healer who uses a remarkably strong form of visualisation to help her patients. She was once trying to heal a cat that had been badly injured in a road accident. The vet said he could do nothing for it and that it should be put down, but Marilyn was convinced she could help it. However, after ten days it was still not responding. Then she sat down and visualised the injured leg as if it were a shattered vase. Slowly, in her mind, she put the pieces together as if she were doing a jigsaw. Then after visualising the leg whole, she mentally put a plaster on it. Within a week the cat, which until then had been unable to walk, was racing around the house.

We specialise so much in today's world that not only do we separate the medical treatment of humans and animals but we specialise within those categories. We are also apt to think that healing, spiritual healing, is something quite apart from orthodox medicine. This is wrong: orthodox healing can be greatly helped by spiritual healing. In fact all the best doctors and vets are healers as well: whether they realise it or not, they give more than their intellectual knowledge to their patients.

We all use healing in our daily lives. When we stroke a sick animal or say to a small child, 'Let me kiss it better!' we are using healing. When our thoughts go out in sympathy and love to someone who is sick we are practising absent healing. When we pray to God and the person or animal seems better for our prayers we think God has done it; but we, by our prayers, have sent out love and healing - by praying we added to the power - but the healing energy, 'the energy of love' as Gordon Turner called it, still comes from ourselves.

A famous veterinary surgeon who was very much a healer as well as an orthodox vet was Buster Lloyd-Jones. He used homeopathy and herbalism in his work, and prayer. He not only prayed himself but got all his staff praying with him.

Following recognition that animals can be helped by people has come a dawning realisation that it works the other way round. Animals can help people! An American gave a name to this, pet therapy. Pet therapy, which has nothing to do with helping animals but with animals helping people, is now used world-wide; cats, as one might guess, are very much a part of this new therapy.

All healers, whatever method they use, are aware of the 'oneness' of Life, of the interaction of living creatures one with another. Pet therapy is a recognition and an application of this, a tapping the life force wherever it exists.

For a long time it has been customary to take flowers to the sick. I think there is more to this than merely bringing something beautiful to brighten up a sickroom. Flowers are alive, they bring their own life force into the room - a tangible source of energy that can be drawn on.

Animals, by contrast, have always been debarred from the sickroom, but now it seems that we are waking up to their potential as healers.

Cat lovers have long known the soothing and relaxing qualities of cats, who have themselves mastered so perfectly the art of relaxation. The professional world is now also coming to recognise this same quality.

Dr Levinson is an American who has written extensively on the subject of pets and mental health, particularly in children. He wrote: 'Animals help to satisfy deep rooted psychological needs in people - they furnish contact comfort, make us feel needed, teach us patience and self-control, and kindness and empathy.' And again: 'Literally a pet can occasionally represent the difference between life and death.'

Strong words - but again something that we who love cats have always known; we can only be amazed that it has taken the world of professional healers and helpers so long to grasp it!

Children and animals usually relate well. The child, before it has received too much conditioning and 'educating' from the adult world, is closer to animals and still thinks much more in a visual rather than a verbal manner, as is the case with animals.

Many of us will have experienced the companionship and comfort of a cat on the bed when we were sick. It probably never occurred to us that what we were getting was more than companionship.

Our cats, as we know, are full of electricity. We can sometimes hear the coat crackle and even receive a shock. As A. Koran wrote in his book *Bring Out the Magic in Your Mind*: 'Electricity attracts, draws things to you: electricity counts. People who are ill in bed and have a cat for company stroke it and stroke it. By stroking the cat they get some of the electricity from its body, and this helps to strengthen them and get them better.'

We think we are giving to our cats when we stroke them, but we could be taking.

Leadbeater, one of the leaders of the Theosophical Society in the early decades of this century, had something to say about the cat's purr. He wrote in one of his books, 'The purring cat surrounds himself with concentric rosy cloud films which expand constantly outward until they dissipate, shedding an influence of drowsy contentment and well-being which tends to reproduce itself in the human beings about him.'

How true! I know of no sound in the world, no music even, so truly relaxing as the steady thrum of a contented cat at peace with himself - and everyone else.

There is an old belief that those who habitually sit with a cat on their lap suffer less from rheumatism and allied ailments than other people; certainly cats themselves never seem to get rheumatism or arthritis, even in old age. In fact cats do not seem to grow old like other creatures. Maybe they sleep a little more and lose a few teeth, but they do not seem to get as hard of hearing, dim of eyes and grey of hair as we and many other animals do in old age.

The University of Pennsylvania held a conference a few years ago on the human-animal companion bond. This attracted some 500 or so interested people, representing various viewpoints - anthropologists and animal behaviourists, veterinarians, psychologists and psychiatrists, all anxious to study the importance of pet animals in relation to human health.

This conference was a milestone in the development of our relations with the animal world - an admission that we had something to learn from them, that there was more to animals and that they had more to give us than their physical bodies for food, clothing or even work.

As a result of scientific investigation we now know for a fact what many of us have been sure of for a long time: that animals really do heal. Not only do we feel relaxed when our cat settles purring in our lap, or we stroke our dog when it comes to sit close to us, but we are more relaxed. Our blood pressure actually drops.

A study of patients returning home after serious heart surgery showed that those who returned to beloved pets had a considerably higher survival rate than those who did not.

In 1975 Dr Leo Bustad, a Washington veterinarian, started a scheme which he called 'Bustad's People/Pet Partnership Program'. Like many good ideas it started almost by accident.

His mother was sick in hospital and to cheer her up he smuggled her little dog in to visit her. He was amazed at the reaction from the other patients. Many wanted to touch the dog. 'As if, he said 'they were starving for some contact'.

He went home thinking about it. The result was his scheme to place animals in hospitals and homes for the sick and elderly on a permanent basis. The first one to be so placed was a cat who took up permanent residence in a nursing home. The experiment was so successful that it was extended to other homes and hospitals.

'The beauty of animals', Dr Bustad said, 'is that they make no judgements. They are always accepting and they don't care how you look.'

Cats would appear to be particularly suited to this work with their inborn ability to look after themselves (they don't need or expect to be taken for walks) and their knowledge and use of total relaxation.

Gussie, daughter of dear old Muggins and my first ever white cat, the one who started me off on the fascinating road that led to the equally fascinating world of pedigree cats, was a tremendous personality with a great love for people. She loved me, she loved everyone in the family, but best of all she loved my father and would sit with him every evening.

Because, dearly as I loved her, I wasn't really her favourite person, I left her with my parents when I left home and later when I married. She was twelve years old when my father died, quite an old lady in cat terms, and because she had loved him and he her, my mother took her to live with her when the family home was sold after his death and she moved to a small house in town.

It was quite a change for a cat who had lived all her life in the country, but she settled perfectly and gave my mother five more years of loving companionship before dying at the ripe old age of seventeen.

My mother always claimed that she 'didn't really like cats', but always qualified this with, 'There are one or two, mind you, that I've grown very fond of-Tiny, and Gussie'.

Even so I was amazed when I learned that Gussie not only shared her home - but her bed. Quite a remarkable feat on the old cat's part. I learned this when my mother told me this amusing story.

Mother had recently had a bad bout of flu and the doctor had visited her at home while she was in bed. She also suffered from arthritis in her knees, but was somewhat taken aback when, without a word, the doctor suddenly swept the bed clothes back to look at her knees. There, down the bed, against her leg, warmer than any hot-water bottle, was Gussie.

'I don't know who was the most surprised - the doctor or Gussie', 'she said; 'I know I felt rather foolish!'

130

Man and cat, she told me, just looked at one another for what seemed a very long minute. Then he silently replaced the bedclothes without making any comment.

Gussie, she admitted, habitually slept there, adding somewhat defensively when she saw my amazement that she was sure it was good for her arthritis. I was sure it was too; I was merely amazed at Gussie's achievement, for my mother had always only allowed cats in my sisters' and my bedrooms under sufferance

Though many of the kittens I bred went as pets to lonely people, only one - Caroline, a white daughter of Tiny - was bought specifically for therapeutic purposes.

She was purchased at ten weeks old by a policeman for his wife who was an invalid and bed bound. When he came and chose her, and told me what he wanted her for I was a little worried and even demurred about selling her to him. Not that I felt it would be a bad home for Caroline, but I felt a ten-week-old kitten would not be serious and responsible enough for such a job. I thought his wife would be better with an older cat.

He told me that he wanted something cheerful and frivolous to brighten up her life. I finally let her go with a promise from him that if she proved too young and frivolous he would return her.

Three months later he phoned me. Caroline was a huge success. She and his wife had taken to one another instantly and she spent almost all the time with his wife providing amusement, company and boundless affection. She was 100 per cent a success and his wife seemed not only much happier but better in herself since she had her.

I was delighted. Caroline had been, not the runt of the litter (her sister Candy, microscopic at birth, had been that), but certainly the plain one - not up to breeding or show standard.

That she proved to have such a wonderful temperament and was such a success in the far more important role of companion was very satisfactory. That is all I thought then. Now I think that it also says something about breeding animals for show qualities only - are we doing them a great disservice?

I was recently told of another white cat, a beautiful Persian lady called Carlotta, whose mistress had been an active social worker of the voluntary kind. Carlotta, she said, could have been a registered hospital aide (only this was in the days when the idea of animals in hospitals was quite taboo). She always knew when to be playful and distracting, and take a person's mind off their troubles. Or when to jump onto laps and purr, and give hypnotic pussy eye therapy. Small children forgot their troubles as they hugged her tightly or brushed out her long fur.

Her mistress was widowed when Carlotta was still only a kitten. Even so, she understood enough to creep up the stairs that first dreadful lonely night and occupy the awful empty space on the other side of the bed, trying desperately, it seemed, to fill the whole room with her purr.

In her book *Animals Are Equal: An Exploration of Animal Consciousness*, Rebecca Hall tells of many cats who are healers. One of these is a cat called Girlie who belongs to healer Arthur Johnson and his wife. Arthur believes that cats are of a high vibration and therefore very good for humans to have near them.

Arthur and his wife treat about seventy patients a week in the healing sanctuary at their home. Girlie usually sits in the room where the patients are waiting and often sits on the lap of someone and prepares them to receive healing. These people invariably report being soothed and helped by her.

Another noted healing cat is Electra, a Siamese living in a healing centre in New York. One person who had stayed at the centre for treatment for stomach trouble said that whenever the pain came on Electra seemed to know and jumped on her lap; immediately she felt a warm glow and the pain just seemed to melt away.

Kay Hogg, a Theosophist and healer, had a Burmese for many years, Coffee Cat, who also appeared to have healing powers. One particular instance was a man who came down to see her from Scotland suffering from a bad ulcerous condition of the legs. As he sat in an armchair one afternoon Coffee Cat settled down on his right foot and refused to move. Later that evening the man and his wife returned to Scotland and three days later wrote to say that his right leg was completely healed. Though he had slight trouble afterwards with the left leg, the right never gave him any trouble again.

Cats are often a great help to people in emotional trouble. It is quite impossible not to feel some comfort, some lift of the spirit, when a cat settles purring on your lap.

We often think how odd it is that cats so frequently go to people and rub around them, even jump on their laps, when they profess a dislike, even a hatred of cats.

Perhaps the cat in these instances really knows better. The avowed cat hater is in some inner turmoil and actually needs healing from the cat. That may sound an outlandish idea, but surely not more so than to believe that the cat, in every other respect so intelligent and so sensitive, should habitually make such a monumental blunder.

Those who live with both dogs and cats will know that whereas dogs choose dog lovers to favour with their attention, cats frequently pick out the one person in the room who insists they dislike cats to rub around them or even settle on their laps.

Cats have a strange way of coming into a person's life when most needed. Tiny came to me when I was at a low ebb emotionally, psychically and spiritually. She stayed with me for ten years through many ups and downs, and left me when I no longer had the same emotional need of her. Many cat lovers I have talked to have had the same feeling about particularly beloved cats in their lives.

Kitty was another white cat, a daughter of old Gussie. As a kitten she had cat flu very badly and though she recovered, one eye remained closed in a permanent wink, giving her an odd and rakish expression. I gave her to an elderly friend who had just come through a bad time nursing an even older relative until her death. She was now alone in the little cottage they had shared.

Kitty mitigated the emptiness and loneliness and, more importantly, gave Mary someone else to think about - to care for. She told me that many a time she probably wouldn't have bothered to get a meal just for herself after years of thinking for someone else, but Kitty demanded hers - and while you were feeding one, well, you might as well feed two!

The expanding use of cats and other animals in hospitals and other institutions, even prisons, throughout the world is proof of their power to heal sickness of the body or mind.

Knowing my interest in the subject a friend recently sent me a newspaper clipping showing an appallingly burnt child playing with a kitten at the Moody State School in Galveston, Texas. The kitten was an important part of the therapy programme for injured children.

An essential part of healing is love and acceptance; in fact if they are absent in the healer there can be no healing.

The following delightful little poem about acceptance was written by June York-Moore after seeing a small Down's

Syndrome child and a cat curled up together in an old armchair.

The poem is called 'Acceptance' and was first published in *Animal Friends* magazine.

There she sat
With a cat
Tucked under her chin:
In the arms
Of a soft old chair

Till the cat
With a very nice smile
Seemed to say,
'Oh stay for while. sweet Sarah;
For I do not mind
If your little mind
 Can never be whole like the others
Who ruffle my fur
And often incur
My wrath
When they tickle my whiskers.
So Sarah stayed there Just a few minutes more,
Content with the gentle Mignon:
Who gave her
Not only a very nice smile -
But also, the warmth of acceptance.

The gift of soothing company, true companionship and real acceptance is healing indeed.

Chapter 11
Cat Character

This chapter was to have been called 'Cat Characters', but as I typed the words I realised that I could not possibly pick out one or two cats of my acquaintanceship and so label them: all cats are characters. So I left off the final 's' and decided to talk about that most fascinating of subjects (to a cat lover) - cat character.

As a character the cat is fascinating. Not only is she the only animal domesticated by man that has not been made useful, neither as a beast of burden nor as a producer of clothing and food, but she is also the only one who, although domesticated. can still if necessary fend perfectly well for herself in the wild.

Two things will immediately stand out to a serious observer of cats. First their undoubted intelligence; second, the fact that. they are quite amoral. It is these two factors taken together that make the cat almost impossible to train in the sense that we can train a horse or a dog.

She is far too intelligent to repeat ad nauseam boring routines just for the food reward at the end, doubly so when her lack of moral sense encourages her to steal what she wants anyway! Though as the cat herself would say, and as many cat lovers would agree. cats do not steal - they merely help themselves to what they consider theirs anyway!

One of the characteristics of the cat that undoubtedly attracts people to her, and having attracted draws forth a devotion that often borders on worship, is that air about the cat of knowing perfectly well that once upon a time she was worshipped. She still expects it; and in the way that we all tend to be treated as we think people will treat us, she gets devotion.

The dog on the other hand expects to give devotion and humbly hopes to be loved a little in return. But not for puss the ingratiating tail wag, the ecstatic welcome home or heart-rending sobbing when you leave.

Such restraint has resulted in her being labelled cold, selfish and unaffectionate. An unfair label? 'Yes', will be the emphatic answer of all of us who love cats and believe we are loved in return.

I have said the cat is almost impossible to train to do tricks. Almost but not quite. Cats can be persuaded to perform.

About forty years ago I was on holiday with my family in Blackpool. While there we went to the famous Tower Circus and on the programme was an act I have never forgotten because it was so unique. In fact it was billed as the 'only performing cats in the world.'

To me this troupe of some ten or so perfectly ordinary domestic cats who ran quite freely into the ring with their young and glamourous girl trainer were far more enjoyable and exciting than the act of their larger cousins, the lions and tigers, performing under restraint behind bars.

I have never seen such an act again, and over the years I have often wondered what particular gift this girl had to persuade them to perform so splendidly.

I have had two cats who have happily and willingly performed the same little trick for me. Tiny, my dear little odd-eyed white cat of yesteryear and Sheba, my yellow-eyed white cat of today. The trick is simple enough: jumping through the hoop made of my arms and clasped hands held some feet above the ground.

I consciously taught Tiny to do this, but cannot remember ever giving the same attention to teaching Sheba; it is interesting that of all the cats I have had in a lifetime only two have done this, Tiny and the cat who I was convinced when I first saw her, was her returning spirit in a new body.

They shared another achievement too: a passion for yeast tablets, which Sheba takes from the jar with her left paw. Tiny also did this, and in fact once did an advertisement for Kitzyme, the company that makes them; her fee was about a year's supply of their products. In the advertisement she was photographed helping herself to the tablets with her left paw. Careful observation of my cats has led me to the conclusion that left-handedness, or left-pawedness, occurs in cats in about the same ratio that it does in humans.

But it is more than these skills, more than the similarity of the white coat that makes me feel that in Sheba I have my beloved Tiny back again. It is something in the core, the essence of her - it is her basic character betrayed by her mannerisms that is so similar.

One of the hardest things for us humans to accept about cats is their independence, and the fact that they are capable of looking after themselves.

I never could believe this about Tiny - probably because as a cat she seemed such a fool, though extraordinarily intelligent in 'human' ways! When she climbed trees, she inevitably got stuck if she went up much further than the height from which she could leap to the ground, and when she didn't actually get stuck she slithered to the ground in the most ungainly, awkward and unsafe-looking way I have ever seen. She never hunted, and so of course never caught anything in her life. Actually that is not strictly true. I was writing in my room one afternoon when I was distracted by a loud miaow from the floor. Tiny was sitting gazing at me, shouting to attract my attention, with something beneath her paw. As I knelt down by her she raised her paw, and away fluttered a large moth - unhurt!

I cannot believe that Sheba can look after herself and always try to see she is in at night. Occasionally she outwits me. Admittedly she has a slightly better track record for mousing than Tiny, but she seems to live in her own dreamy white-cloud world and the words of the vet who attended her when I found her lying, more dead than alive, at the drive gate, still ring in my ears:

'She's such a helpless sort of a cat - she could never fend for herself!' All cats live at least two lives simultaneously. Their life with people, where they can be cosy and cossetty and cuddly as can be, and their deep, secret cat life where they become the lone hunter, the deadly predator.

The present-day cat who causes me most qualms with her dual personality is undoubtedly Tabitha. Of all the cats, she is the greatest loner - with the other cats. In one way this is surprising, for she was born one of a large family of kittens and didn't leave her birthplace until she was about ten weeks old, when she came to live with us. She was acquired as a companion for Lucy, a stray kitten of about the same age we had recently adopted, and of course we had our usual complement of older cats. All her life Tabitha has lived with other cats so it is surprising in one way that she is such a loner among them. In another it is not at all surprising: she brought it on herself.

At first she and Lucy were great friends, but as they grew to adolescence it became obvious that they were no longer friends at all. Tabitha was constantly teasing and tormenting Lucy who became terrified of her.

This of course was quite disastrous in every way, for not only did Tabitha tease Lucy more but she began doing the same to the older cats. She became insufferable, swaggering about with her long Siamese tail upright, swinging her hips and shouting at them all in gutter Siamese.

I remember one day she was on one of her favourite look-out spots, perched on the top of a tall gum tree stump in the garden; from this elevated perch she was holding a conversation with my son Graham and me down below, when her roving eye suddenly spotted a white blob moving across the distant paddock towards the house. She stopped talking to us in mid-yowl, almost flew out of the tree and sped across the paddock, her tail now like a large bottle brush.

Poor Sheba, well aware she could never make it to the security of the house without being ignominiously bowled over in the grass, headed back to the creek and her own special hidey-hole.

Then we moved to our present home, only five miles distant. The move was a prolonged one. John and I drove two of the donkeys over in their carts, and stayed for a night; we took Tabitha (in her travelling case) and she spent a blissful twenty-four hours exploring the new home and being an 'only cat'. Poor Tabitha, nemesis was just around the corner.

The move to the new home had a surprising effect on the morale of the other cats. Something about the place seemed to change them all. One by one, they called Tabitha's bluff and found she was only a paper tiger after all. Her days of swaggering about terrorising everyone had gone for ever - even the timid and easily deflated Lucy was no longer afraid of her. Worst of all, Sheba, whom she had bashed up so successfully and kept away from the house for days at a time by the simple process of lying in wait to pounce on her as she made her run across the paddock, turned the tables on her. with the move to the new house a new confidence came over Sheba. I may have unwittingly helped in this: anxious that she should not find another secret hidey-hole like her old one in the creek bank, maybe this time in the Whipstick Forest which surrounds us, I took particular care to give Sheba a great deal of love and attention. She stayed around the house much more. Tabitha we saw much less.

I was quite amazed when I was writing early one morning, at around six, to see Sheba driving Tabitha away from the house - not once, but several times. The tables had certainly turned! Angry as I had been so often in the past when I saw Tabitha driving Sheba away, I could not help feeling sorry for the erstwhile swaggering tease and bully when I saw her being chased away with ignominity!

Maybe it was seeing the change in Sheba's attitude that bolstered Lucy's resolve, but with the move to this house she ceased to run or scream for mercy and help every time Tabitha fixed her with her lime green eyes. The two older cats, Fluffy and Tiger, who had never allowed Tabitha to boss them, became more domineering. Even little Dana, the tabby kitten Ruth picked up abandoned in the middle of Bendigo as a microscopic kitten at about three weeks old, metaphorically cocked a snook at her.

It was almost as if the cats themselves had held a council meeting and resolved that from now on, no one must allow Tabitha to boss them; quite the reverse, they would unite to keep her in order!

Dana herself is an interesting study of cat character. Of all the many cats who have kept me company down the years, none has been so tough as Dana. She appears to be quite fearless and utterly confident of her own worth and importance. From the moment Ruth heard her screaming with all the power of her little self and brought her home, and no doubt before, she has been dedicated to survival. She eats anything and everything whenever and wherever she can, guarding her own food with ferocious growls and unsheathed claws, stealing other people's whenever possible.

She plays rough-and-tumble games with the dogs and the squeaks of pain are always theirs; she calmly commandeers the best cat beds with no thought of sharing.

When she first joined the family she slept in a huge cardboard packing box in Ruth's room. This made a 'pen' from which she could not escape. As she grew in strength and agility, however, it no longer served this useful purpose. She developed the trying habit of sleeping until midnight or one in the morning, then getting up to play energetic and enthusiastic games round the room, punctuated by periods of sucking and nibbling Ruth's neck - another trying habit she had developed, probably as a result of being taken away from her mother and weaned far too young.

Finally, even my cat-adoring daughter announced she could stand these disturbed nights no longer. Dana would be demoted from her bedroom to the laundry already occupied at night by Lucy. To Ruth's chagrin Dana saw this as promotion, not demotion: she looked cheerfully round her new quarters, sampled both beds, settled firmly in the middle of the better one (Lucy's) and went to sleep. Lucy protested in very strong cat language, totally ignored by Dana, and told me in tragic terms what she thought of the arrangement and spent the night on the windowsill.

'To think', Ruth expostulated, 'I've put up with her awful behaviour night after night, with never a decent night's sleep, because I didn't like to turn her out and hurt her feelings - and she actually prefers sleeping in the laundry!'

Many people find it hard to come to terms with the essential duality of cats. Their undoubted psychic powers, their spirituality, and what they see as the 'cruel carnivorous' nature of the physical cat.

Jon Wynne-Tyson, in his book *The Civilised Alternative* dealing with a vegetarian or vegan way of life, touches on this and puts forward the suggestion that as humans change there could be a psychic change within the animal kingdom and that in the future the vegan cat may not be such a far-fetched notion!

I would agree there; many years ago I was a vegetarian from economic necessity - not, as today, from conviction and choice. In those days I was struggling to support both myself and Tiny, my cat, on my somewhat meagre earnings as a freelance journalist. Tiny lived on breakfast cereal and milk, baked beans (which she loved), vegetable soup, and sometimes the real luxury of a tin of sardines or pilchards shared between us. She appeared to enjoy her food and was healthier than at any other period of her life. The eczema that plagued her through the years disappeared. Alas, in more affluent days and a return to a 'better' diet it recurred.

We humans like to think of ourselves as the only species to have advanced beyond what we call 'animal nature'; yet we are the most blatantly carnivorous of all creatures, without even the excuse that the cat has, that we are physiologically designed to eat meat! We do not have the short bowel, the correct jaw formation, the sharp teeth or even the retractable claws of the true carnivore. Those who condemn the cat for her carnivorous habits are often in fact very materialistic in their outlook and, while condemning the cat for eating birds, happily consume 'factory' reared chickens who, unlike the birds killed by the cat, have never lived a life worth living at all.

What so many 'nature lovers' overlook is that it is a fact of life - or of nature - for one living thing to prey on another to survive. To condemn cats for eating birds while at the same time approving of their catching so-called vermin, rats and mice, is totally illogical; particularly while we ourselves adopt a preying and carnivorous lifestyle.

To make a real study of cat character, it is probably necessary to have a family of cats in order to see not only the differences but how they react to one another: who likes who, who bullies who - the pecking order, and how it is established and maintained.

Cat watching in fact can be a very entertaining occupation. Kit and Dana, the two youngest cats, had Tabitha bailed up behind the wheel of a bike that was propped up against the wall one day. They were lying a few feet away from her, eyes glittering with mischievous excitement, tails twitching. Tabitha, trying hard to appear unconcerned, was washing herself vigorously. Into this little tableau walked Fluffy; around the corner of the house. She paused, looked from Tabitha to the other two, and took in the situation at a glance. She promptly sat down. Tabitha visibly froze. Kit and Dana teasing her was one thing: Fluffy she knew, did not play games.

I was on my way into the house through the laundry door with the clothes basket. Tabitha looked at me, waited till I reached the door, then made a run for it. Dana had already been distracted by a butterfly, Kit got up and strolled off, bored, but Fluffy bounded after her and took up her stance on the doorstep where she could see Tabitha coming out before she was seen. She waited. After a short time inside, of course the mercurial Tabitha wanted out. She came to the door, saw Fluffy and ran back in. Fluffy continued to wait. Tabitha watched me carefully; when I was ready to carry the next load of washing out she made a dash for it at the moment when I was between her and Fluffy.

Fluffy twitched her tail, arranged her whiskers and stalked off. It had been quite a satisfactory incident: she had managed to terrorise Tabitha without lifting a paw or in any way jeopardising her own dignity.

It is commonly supposed that the characteristics and character of cats are quite different in every respect to that of dogs. This I think is far from true.

Dogs do not always display unwavering devotion and loyalty, while cats do not have a monopoly on selfishness. Dogs can show as much concern for their creature comforts as cats, and cats can harbour as deep a love for 'their' people as dogs can.

Dogs have learned that it pays to flatter us; cats that it is better to make us flatter them!

People with Siamese cats often say that they like them because they are like dogs! If that is so, why not keep a dog in the first place? I have even heard people say that the only cats they like are Siamese 'because they are not like cats'!

How they delude themselves - Siamese are *all* cat, the very archetype of cat. Everything we think of as cat is there: the cossetty pet cat, the tearer and render, the cool calculating cat, the- loving friend.

The Siamese epitomises the tiger at the hearth, the lion on the mat; anyone who acquires a Siamese because they think it is like a. dog is going to be rapidly educated by the cat! Of course these people who think their Siamese cats are like dogs may have known only dogs like cats. There are quite a few about: dogs who calmly hog the best chair; dogs who can be coolly and calculatingly indifferent when it suits them; dogs who refuse to be bossed. If any breed of dog can claim to be more like cats than any other it is probably the Pekinese. They even look rather like Persian cats.

To say a cat is dog-like is usually meant as a compliment (though I doubt very much if many cats would see it in that light). If a cat trots after us around the place, we say she is following us 'like a dog'. Yet the plain fact is that cats are often just as willing to walk around with us as dogs. Being on the whole so much smaller, however, they are not so keen on long tramps as dogs.

But when Ruth or I go across the paddock to the vegetable garden or down the drive to get the mail, or any other little sortie about the property, we usually have cats accompanying us as a matter of course.

In fact, quite often, when we are leaving the property we have to shut the cats in to make sure they don't follow us! Graham and I were riding one morning; we had crossed the paddock from the house and were going up the road at a brisk trot with two of the dogs accompanying us. Graham happened to glance back over his shoulder and immediately reined in his horse.

'Look!' he said to me.

I stopped and looked back. Running up the hill, pink mouth opening in a loud mew of 'wait for me - I'm coming!' was Sheba. Right in the middle of the road - which, thank goodness is a reasonably quiet country one. Had it not been, I dread to think what might have happened to her, for she was oblivious to anything but the need to catch us up!

We turned round and rode back. She followed us home and I shut her in the house. What a funny little cavalcade we would have presented to any passer-by! I was riding Pepita, my little twelve-hand mule; Graham, in shorts and barefoot, was riding Talisman, his sixteen-hand horse, and we were accompanied by a large German Shepherd, another large dog of unknown parentage (muzzled because of her unfortunate habit of biting first and asking questions afterwards) and a white cat, who herself presented a somewhat bizarre appearance; normally long-haired, she had been freshly clipped for the summer, all but a tennis ball size pom-pom on the end of her tail!

Though Sheba followed me around the house and garden it had never occurred to me that she would actually follow the horses. Since then, however, I make sure she is inside when I set off for a ride!

Kit is another little cat who is often described as doglike. She trots after people with enthusiasm; rests in a peculiar manner, chin on the floor in front of her, like a dog; does dreadful doglike things such as pulling up freshly planted things in the garden, then rolling on them; and odd things, for a cat, like rolling ecstatically on soaking newly hosed concrete. She has a lousy sense of balance and can fall off a gatepost that any self-respecting cat could balance on with the greatest of ease.

I often say she must have been a dog the last time around and she hasn't got used to the new body, but the explanation could be a deal simpler. When Ruth bought her she was in a pen in the pet shop with puppies, and when she was still a kitten RuTh acquired a puppy herself. Zoe and Kit spent many hours together, playing rough-and-tumble - games that were an odd mixture of puppy and kitten play, during which she absorbed, no doubt, a good many dog ways.

One reason often put forward to substantiate the claim that Siamese are doglike is that they are easy to teach to walk on a lead. Well, all 1 can say to that is that I have had several cats in my life of various breeds and mixtures who have learned to walk beautifully on a lead.

Honey, my Abyssinian, was one (Abyssinians are usually thought of as being pure cat). The first Tabitha was another, but Tabitha Two, who is part Siamese, totally and absolutely refuses to walk on a leash. I put this down not to stupidity but to very calculating catlike brains. When I put the harness and lead on her, I think her mind ticks over something like this:

'Now, if I ever so much as take one step willingly in this contraption, she'll have me in it all the time - I'll never be free again!'

She never has taken so much as one step in it. Her legs simply dissolve into jelly and she collapses in a boneless heap on the floor. I have even tried ignoring this and walking anyway~ but she drags along behind me like an old toy that has lost most of its stuffing - she does not walk!

This does not mean that we never use the lead. She wears it when she goes out in the car, when she enjoys sitting looking out of the window. The harness and lead means that whoever is holding her has a reasonably secure grip in case of emergency. She wore it when we took her to an 'animals visiting day' at the local home and hospital for the aged. It was a good thing too, because as it turned out she was the only cat (three tiny kittens in a wire basket could barely be counted) among a large gathering of dogs. Without The security that the harness gave both her and Ruth she would undoubtedly have shinned up the nearest tall tree to shout abuse at the dogs from the safety of its branches. As it was she remained securely in Ruth's arms and was very gracious and polite to the old people, many of whom found great pleasure in stroking her and talking to her.

The character of cats, like that of people, varies so enormously from one individual to another that I think it is as difficult to say categorically, 'Cats do this - or that', or 'cats are like s~and-so', as it is to say so about people. Certainly they cannot be classified by breed any more than people can by race.

It is as much a common misconception that all Persians are stately, cossetty cats as it is to say all Siamese are doglike. The only certain thing that can be said about cats is that no two are quite alike. However, underlying the differences and binding Them together there are certain characteristics, or tendencies, that at least most cats share - even if it is only their fierce determination to be individuals!

One of these is undoubtedly their self-possession; it is a quality That smacks both of dignity and mysticism. Deep down we all know that though we may not be able to live without cats, cats on the other hand could perfectly well live without us.

A characteristic that all cats have in common is a determination not to lose face. It is probably this as much as an obsession with cleanliness that makes them wash so often. Whenever in danger of losing her dignity a cat will wash. She will do it with great concentration, as if this had been her sole intention all along. A very convenient face- saver, the wash!

Dignity is all-important to most cats and therefore it follows that if we want to keep their friendship we must respect this and do our best not to make them look foolish. Are they so different from us - after all who does like looking a fool?

Washing, of course, is not only a face-saver. Cats are particular, even vain, about their personal appearance.

I spent one summer sharing a tiny terraced house in Barnes, London with my sister. The house was right on the pavement and on the other side of the road was the river. The ground-floor rooms were slightly below street level, which meant that our sitting room on the next floor was not so high above the pavement. The window was only just above the heads of passers-by.

Each evening Tiny installed herself in the window in the evening sun. At first we thought it was to enjoy the sun and admire the magnificent view across the Thames. After a while we began to wonder if she wasn't there to be admired, rather than admire!

As we sat in the room, out of sight of passers-by, we would hear footsteps stopping and often a voice speaking to Tiny or saying to a companion something like, 'Oh, do look! What a pretty little cat!'

When this happened Tiny invariably drew herself up slightly and responded to the admirer with a small 'prrt!' of acknowledgement, then looked across the room at us to make sure we had seen and heard.

On the subject of washing, cats can use the wash not only to save face but to be thoroughly insulting. Invariably a mother cat will thoroughly scrub her kittens clean if a human hand has touched them. And how often does a cat turn round and wash the very spot where she has been stroked by a doting owner? The message given (and received, unless the owner is very thick) is all too plain!

Donkeys have, often quite unreservedly, a reputation for being stubborn. The phrase 'stubborn as a cat' is never heard, yet if it comes to sheer obstinate determination there is nothing to beat a cat.

When a cat has decided to rest in a certain chair, there she will rest, and as many times as she is lifted off she will get back on again. I am sure I am not the only cat lover who will choose another chair in the room rather than the one the cat wants!

Sheba is particularly persistent i'n the matter of her resting places, and the trying part is that she often chooses such odd places: on top of the fridge, or worse, inside the pantry- quite a convenient place for her, for if she happens to wake up feeling hungry she could help herself to a snack of dog biscuits! Fortunately, the recent move to the new house has stopped this because I no longer have a walk-in pantry! When she has a fixation for a certain resting place, nothing will change it: as often as she is moved she will go back there. And since she seems to spend some twenty-three hours out of twenty-four either sleeping or resting (or somewhere off on the astral plane) she has a good deal more time and energy than I have.

This obstinacy of the cat can of course be termed patience and determination when it is used to what we call 'good effect' that is, keeping our homes free of mice. There is no more chilling glance in all the world than that given by a cat keeping vigil at a mousehole when a great stupid lumbering human comes on the scene.

The character of a cat is as hard to pin down as a shaft of moonlight, and some would say as cold. But this is no real mystery. The truth of the matter is that cats are just like people. Maybe that is what their detractors see in them - human faults and failings, their own maybe, mirrored in a furry form?

Sometimes cool and calculating, sometimes warm and loving; sometimes stately, sometimes frivolous; a ball of energy or disgustingly lazy; usually looking after number one yet occasionally capable of touching and selfless love; sometimes as timid as a mouse, a scaredy-cat, sometimes as brave as a lion.

As in us, there is a little bit of bad in the best of them and a little bit of good in the worst of them; they are really very human - perhaps that is why we love them!

Chapter 12
Cats Between Covers

There seems to be a natural empathy between cats and writers, perhaps because writing is a solitary introspective profession and cats are solitary introspective creatures. Many famous writers down the ages have been passionate cat lovers.

In nineteenth-century France the many writers who were devotees of the cult of the cat (Gautier, Victor Hugo, Baudelaire, Anatole France, Zola) did much to raise the status of cats in general, not only in their own country but in Europe as a whole.

Theophile Gautier, who wrote a great deal about his own cats, said of Baudelaire and his cats: 'With admirable patience they wait until he has finished his task, emitting a guttural and rhythmic purr as a sort of accompaniment to his work~. About his own cats Gautier wrote: 'They like silence, order and quietness and no place is so proper for them as the study of a man of letters'. Maybe it is cats who are writer lovers more than writers who are cat lovers?

Gautier himself had two white cats, Don Pierrot de Navarre, who shared his bed, and Seraphita. His devotion to these two bordered on worship. They were his constant companions and he wrote with them, and about them. Of Seraphita: 'She was of a dreamy and contemplative disposition. She would sit on a cushion for hours together, quite motionless, not asleep and following with her eyes, in a rapture of attention, sights invisible to mere mortals.'

When Pierrot fell sick Gautier did all he could for him, even procuring special supplies of asses' milk, alas to no avail. He was buried beneath a white rose tree in the garden and three years later Seraphita was laid to rest by him.

Emile Zola too appears to have had a particular penchant for white cats, for they often appear in his books. Minouche of La Joie de Vivre was described as 'a little white cat with delicate airs whose tail twitched at the sight of mud'.

Cats stalk through the pages of many great works of fiction. There are three cats in Dickens' *Bleak House*, and an old cat befriends the little Paul Dombey in *Dombey & Son*. Dickens describes this cat as it lay in the lender 'purring egotistically . . while the contracting pupils of his eyes looked like two notes of admiration.'

Colette, the famous French novelist, was renowned for her love of animals and birds and was particularly fond of cats. In fact one of her novels has a cat, Saha, as the principal character. The book is called *La Chatte*. Saha is a short-haired blue cat, in the original French described as a Chartreuse, the French name for the breed known in England as the British Blue. In the English translation of the novel, however, she is described as a Russian Blue. British or Russian, she is so well evoked by Colette that one can almost hear her purring through the pages of the book.

Writing about their own cats was not limited to the French writers on the nineteenth century. Michael Joseph's *Charles* has become something of a classic in cat books.

Bruce Marshall took time off from writing his very successful novels to write a little book about the cats in his life, *Thoughts of My Cats*, in which he admits that he has always preferred them to dogs, and even to most humans. He considered them 'dignified, unaffected and sincere':

Cats... are among the few neighbours I have been able to love outside the Lord. I don't need to drink myself half-silly in order to listen to their anecdotal chatter, and they don't require to anaesthetize themselves against me. They don't mind my shortcomings; and I don't think that they have any.

One of the better-known twentieth-century writers and cat lovers is Paul Gallico. He writes with humour - and great understanding - of the many cats who have shared his life. There was one memorable period when, as he says, 'I was doing the bidding of some twenty- three assorted felines all at the same time,'

He loves cats dearly, but is not fooled for one minute by their manipulative powers:

'Of all things a smart cat does to whip you into line, the gift of the captured mouse is the cleverest and most touching... You can teach a dog to retrieve and bring you game, but only a cat will voluntarily hand over its kill to you as an unsolicited gift - and makes you her slave - ever after. Once you have been presented with a mouse by your cat, you will never be the same again. She can use you for a doormat. And she will, too!

Beverley Nichols was well known for his love of cats. His *Cats A.B.C.* is something of a classic among cat books. Writing in this about one of his cats, Oscar, he says that he has a morbid craving for olives, which have to be kept locked up before a party. He goes on to say: 'in any place where cat lovers are gathered together, sooner or later the subject of food will be eagerly discussed with particular emphasis on any pussy who has peculiar tastes.'

How right he was, because cats are supposed to be carnivorous hunters, and any cat with odd and individual tastes invariably remains clearly etched in one's memory. 'When I was young we had a pretty little blue and white cat called Dinky. A quiet little cat there is not much that sticks in my memory about her except her passion for nuts, a passion shared by my father. He could never, it seemed, help himself to a nut from the bowl or collect the nutcrackers without Dinky knowing; there she would be sitting in front of him, her eyes fixed on him, her small mouth opening in a pink mew of 'Pretty Please!'

But odd though her taste was it was not quite so bizarre as that of her father, Monty. Monty lived just up the road and belonged to friends of ours. His passion was oranges! 'Whenever an orange was peeled he would sit up on his haunches begging, his eyes fixed unwaveringly on the peeler. Towards the end of his life he was hit by a car and though he recovered he was blind for the remainder of his days. His passion for oranges however was unabated. The minute he caught the delectable scent of one being peeled he was there in front of the peeler, his nose twitching ever so slightly, as he waited in the old begging stance for the slice which he had infinite faith would be forthcoming.

Dear old Tilly had a passion for pumpkin. She had liked marrow in England, but pumpkin, ripened in the Australian sun - that was one of the pleasures worth travelling to the other side of the world for!

Beverley Nichols was quite right! I have digressed - from the subject of 'cats between covers' to the way- out tastes of some of the cats I have known personally.

Probably two of the most famous cats between covers are Solomon and Sheba, the two satanic Siamese made famous by Doreen Tovey in her books *Cats in The Belfry* and *Cats In May*.

Wildly funny, these books are the hilarious accounts of day-to-day life with Siamese cats. When Solomon and Sheba couldn't find enough mischief to get into at home they set off looking for it, and had to be fetched home. She writes:

*You didn't need to look for the reason why people thought
we were nuts ... when practically every day saw us
marching through the village at least once carrying those
wretched cats in public procession. Charles, pink with
embarrassment because the only way Sheba would be
carried was flat on her back in his arms, gazing
adoringly up into his face; I with Solomon dangling
goofily down my back like a sack of coals while I held
onto him by his hind legs. Unless of course it was the fly
season, when, though I still held him by his back legs,
with his front ones he would be flailing the air behind me
like a demented windmill.*

Lloyd Alexander is another writer who put his own cats
between covers in a very well-known book *My Five Tigers*.

One of his cats was called Heathcllff, who just turned up and
decided to live with him when he happened to be reading
Emily Bronte's *Wuthering Heights*. Heathcliff not only took
over the house but Lloyd Alexander as well, organising his
dally timetable to his liking. He was, in contrast to many of his
kind, a 'daytime' cat and heartily disliked his master's habit of
writing at night, so much so that he managed to. reorganise
things by rousing him firmly at six in the morning and
insisting on a nap in the afternoons: 'Gradually I reversed my
original programme - working through the day and taking
meals at normal human hours, I accomplished just as much,
and made both Janine and Heathcllff considerably happier.'

If anyone doubts the power of a cat to order the routine of a
person, or even a household, then all I can say is he has never
lived with a determined cat!

If you are foolish enough to share your sleeping
accommodation with a cat, and that cat wants to get up at six,
then at six it will get up, and so will you! If there is no pressing
reason to be up early you may crawl back between the sheets
and snatch a few more hours of sleep, but you will get up when

the cat says, because there is no more persistent alarm clock than a wakeful cat!

It is only in retrospect that I appreciate Tiny's remarkable ability to wake me at the correct time - early if I wished to be early, late if I wanted to sleep in - by simply sitting very close to my head and staring at me. If only Tabitha would do the same today! But no, whenever Tabitha wants to get up, which may be any time between two and seven, she sits by my head - but not silently: she talks 'pidgin Siamese' in my ear and starts kneading my head with claws out!

Heathcliff's method was somewhat different. But none the less effective. Lloyd Alexander writes: 'Although he never budged no matter how much I tossed him about during the night, I was fair game whenever I slept late in the mornings ... If I made the slightest move in my sleep, he would leap to the bed and pounce on me, grappling my feet through the covers or racing back and forth across my stomach ... I began working at six in the morning and starting to bed a little earlier.'

He also gives an amusing account of how Heathcliff curtailed his violin playing, which he had taken up as a hobby and means of relaxation. Heathcliff detested the noise, and wherever he was when he heard it he came and tried to stop it, first by distracting his master's attention by rubbing round his legs and demanding fuss, then by trying to get him to play with a bit of paper; finally, he 'took direct action. Balancing himself on his hind feet, he reached up and sank his claws into my knees. The more I played, the harder he scratched, yowling and growling at the same time. As usual I surrendered to him and cut my practice sessions short. If my wife had him to thank for putting me on a respectable schedule, I'm sure the neighbours were equally gratified by his effect on my musical ambitions!'

Cats, Lloyd Alexander thinks, make an impression on us which we elaborate with our own imaginations. This I think is quite true; they remind us of 'types' of certain people, of characters out of books. Heathcllff, he said, produced an enormous variety of such impressions when he first arrived: 'with his shabby fur, and preposterous swagger' he reminded him of Mr Micawber.

But at bottom, for me he was always Heathcliff. I saw too much wildness in him, with his brooding, gypsy-like aspect, ever to put a great deal of credence in the other roles ... To this day I cannot read the passage, 'his basilisk eyes were nearly quenched', or 'Mr Heathcliff, grim and saturnine', without thinking of my good friend. But I do not feel it has spoiled the book. It has merely given me an unusual approach to the work of Emily Bronte.

One of the most entertaining fictitious cats between covers is surely Webster, the creation of PG. Wodehouse in *Mulliner Nights*.

Webster was a clerical cat, brought up in a Dean's household in a cathedral city. He was 'very large, and very black and very composed ... descendant of a long line of ecclesiastical ancestors ... he had that exquisite poise which one sees in high dignitaries of the church.'

'When his owner was elevated to a bishopric - in Africa - he sent Webster to live with his bohemian artist nephew in London. 'When he arrived, Lancelot. opened the travelling basket and looked into eyes that were 'clear and steady, and seemed to pierce to the very roots of the young man's soul, filling him with a sense of guilt.'

Lancelot, who had been brought up by his uncle, the Dean, remembered an incident from his childhood when he 'had been so carried away by ginger-beer and original sin as to plug a senior canon in the leg with his airgun.' A visiting archdeacon however had witnessed the incident. 'As he felt then when he turned and met the archdeacon's eye, so he felt now as

Webster's gaze played silently upon him. Webster it was true, had not actually raised his eyebrows; but this, Lancelot felt, was simply because he hadn't any.'

Like the real-life Heathcllff, the fictitious Webster reorganised Lancelot's life, almost succeeding in turning him from a casual, untidy, carefree artist into a respectable citizen and a pillar of society. He almost, but not quite, got him to drop his equally bohemian fiancee for some one respectable and eminently dull.

Fortunately for Lancelot, he discovered Webster's Achilles' heel just in time - a liking for strong drink - and so broke the spell of his disapproving eye.

Living as I do in the same house as a cat, my daughter's Fluffy who can give just such a piercing, all-seeing glare of frosty disapproval, I could identify very well with Lancelot and found the story of Webster quite probable.

Aesop, that master storyteller, told many fables about cats. One was of a young man who fell in love with a cat. He prayed to Venus, the goddess of love, to turn her into a woman. He then married his 'cat-girl'. Their happiness, however, was very short-lived, for on their wedding night she saw a mouse and instinctively sprang out of bed after it. Venus, furious, turned her back into a cat again, realising that she had only succeeded in changing her outer form anyway. The advice constantly given by Aesop is that the cat is naturally a predatory beast; it will never cease to have cat-nature, and if we are stupid enough to think it will. then we deserve to be devoured by it. One of the better-known cats between covers is another real-life cat - Dr Johnson's Hodge. James Boswell, in his *Life of Johnson*, writes of him:

> *I never shall forget the indulgence with which Dr Johnson treated Hodge, his cat: for whom he himself used to go out and buy oysters, lest the servants having that trouble should take a dislike to the poor creature. I am,*

unluckily, one of those who have an antipathy to a cat, so that Iam uneasy when in the room with one: and I own, I frequently suffered a good deal from the presence of the same Hodge.

Another eighteenth century cat was an unfortunate church cat which adopted George Borrow in Wales. He writes of it:

As I and my family sat at tea in the parlour, an hour or two after we had taken possession of our lodgings - the door being open on account of the fineness of the weather - a poor black cat entered, sat down on the carpet by the table and mewed piteously. It was dreadfully attenuated, being nothing but skin and bone.

He found out that it had been left behind by a previous vicar of Llangollen whose successor had brought with him cats and dogs that drove it away.

Almost all the people of the town were dissenters, and knowing the cat to be a church cat, they not only would not harbour it, but did all they could to make it miserable. Oh, there never was a cat so persecuted as that poor Church of England animal, and solely on account of the opinions which it was supposed to have imbibed in the house of its late master.

The unfortunate cat had been homeless for two years, and though the cottage in which George Borrow and his family were living adjoined the vicarage grounds, it had never attempted to enter it before; yet within two hours of their moving in, it joined them. George Borrow goes on:

Did instinct draw it towards us? We gave it some bread and butter and a little tea with milk and sugar. it ate and drank and soon began to purr.

The good woman of the house was horrified when on coming to clear the things, she saw the church cat on the carpet. 'What impudence!' she exclaimed, and made towards it, but on our telling her that we did not expect that it should be disturbed, she let it alone.

A very remarkable circumstance was, that though the cat had hitherto been in the habit of flying, not only from her face, but the very echo of her voice, it now looked her in the face with perfect composure, as much as to say, 'I don't fear you for I know that I am now safe with my own people!'

The cat stayed with them and with good food soon began to look 'sleek and bonny' and within less than a week had taken up the habit of sitting on Borrow's shoulders when he was reading or writing. The story had a happy ending, for when they left Llangollen the Borrows found it a home with a 'young woman of sound church principals, who was recently married.' They left it with her along with some 'milk money' and later learned that it lived in peace and comfort until its death.

The cat in fairytale and fiction is often seen as a somewhat cunning helper of man, the two most famous examples of course being Dick Whlttington's cat and Puss in Boots. Though one is an English tale, the other French, the cats in both stories set out to achieve the same end: fame and fortune, and the hand of the fair maiden, for their impoverished masters. Being cats, naturally both succeed.

While there has always been argument about whether Dick Whlttington's cat really existed, Puss in Boots has never been considered anything but fictitious. The story of the delightful swaggering cat, who by dint of great cunning elevated his poor master to such a lofty position, was always my favourite fairy tale, and Puss in Boots the best cat of all!

These are only a few of the cats, live and fictitious, between covers, ln~rose; but cats - who so often keep company with writers - seem to be a splendid source of inspiration for poets too.

Joseph Green, an eighteenth century poet wrote in a lamentation on the death of his cat:

> *How shall I sing? What numbers shall I chuse?*
> *For in my favourite cat I've lost my muse.*

After extolling her virtues for many verses, he continued:-

> *.....we together many evenings sat.*
> *when'er I felt my towering fancy fail,*
> *I stroked her head, her ears, her back and tail;*
> *And as l stroked, improved my dying song*
> *From the sweet notes of her melodious tongue;*
> *Her purrs and mews so evenly kept time,*
> *She purred in metre and she mewed in rhyme.*

Another eighteenth century cat immortalised in verse was William Cowper's *'The Retired Cat'*. This fairly long poem tells how his cat went to sleep in the open drawer which got closed on her. The poem begins with the delightful lines:-

> *A poet's cat, sedate and grave*
> *As poet well could wish to have*

He goes on to tell how she loved to find some spot where she could sit and think, and the most quoted lines of this poem are those which describe one of these, more odd, places:

> *Sometimes her ease and solace sought*
> *In an old empty watering pot,*
> *There wanting nothing but a fan*
> *To seem some nymph in her sedan.*

It was, of course, her love of sitting in odd places that led her to the drawer in the first place, the poem goes on to describe how on finding it open she thought it must be specially for her convenience and settled down comfortably on the linen inside. Unfortunately a maid came into the room, did not see her there, and closed the drawer. She remained there the rest of the day, all night and next day and only the following night were her mews heard and she was released:

> *Forth skipped the cat, not now replete*
> *As erst, with airy self-conceit.*

The last few lines of the poem are the moral of the story and are often quoted alone - (which is a pity, because the rest o~f the poem is so delightful and of course points up the moral):

> *Beware of too sublime a sense*
> *Of your own worth and consequence.*
> *The man who dreams himself so great,*
> *And his importance of such weight,*
> *That all amund in all that's done,*
> *Must move and act for him alone,*
> *Will learn in school of tribulation*
> *The folly of his expectation.*

The descriptive first line of the poem - 'A poet's cat, sedate and grave' - always evokes memories of Tiny for me. Just so could she be described. She would sit like an Egyptian statue on the corner of my desk, gravely watching me type. Occasionally if I spoke to her she would respond with a slight stretching movement and a brief purr, but she never in any way disturbed me.

Not so the first Tabitha: If she got on my desk she could not resist batting a paw at the flying keys or searching for some 'toy' such as a paperclip that she could knock around the desk. Often I would screw up a piece of paper and throw it on the floor for her to play with, only to find that in my desire to distract such a distracting companion, I had screwed up the very sheet I most needed.

William Wordsworth, more famous for his dancing daffodils, wrote a delightful little poem *'The Kitten on the Wall,'* about a kitten playing with autumn leaves. This kitten - apparently also a tabby - is much more like Tabitha:

> *What intenseness of desire*
> *In her upward eye of fire*

He goes on to liken her to an Indian conjuror but says that though she is 'quick as he in feats of art', she is:

> *Far beyond in joy of heart ...*
> *What would little Tabby care*
> *For the plaudits of the crowd?*
> *Over happy to be proud,*
> *Over wealthy in the treasure*
> *Of her own exceeding pleasure.*

Yes, that was certainly my little Tabby: always wealthy in the treasure of her own exceeding pleasure. How happy most of us would be if we could extract the same enjoyment from our lives as she did from hers!

Keats wrote a sonnet, *'To Mrs Reynold's Cat,'* in which are the lines:

> *Gaze*
> *With those bright languid segments green, and prick*
> *those velvet ears - but pr'ythee do not stick*
> *thy latent talons in me*

Lines which I echo many times a day in modern parlance to Tabitha Two. I know only too well that following hard on the gaze of her lime-green eyes and the pricking of her large velvet ears is liable to come the unsheathing of her talons; they will stick into me as her paws begin that odd rhythmic kneading that so often accompanies the thrum of a happy cat's purr.

164

How often do I pull the sheet desperately over my head in the dark early hours of the morning when I hear her wakeful purr throbbing near my eardrums and know, if I haven't already felt them, that next I shall feel those talons working on my head - kneading, and pricking, and 'combing' my sleek tangled hair.

The poets have seen, and caught in words, very clearly the contrasting sides of the cat's character. A.C. Swinburne wrote, in '*To A Cat*':

> *Stately, kindly, lordly friend,*
> *Condescend*
> *Here to sit by me and turn*
> *Glorious eyes that smile and burn.*
> *Golden eyes, love's lustrous meed,*
> *On the golden page I read.*

In the last verse of the poem he apparently refers to the empathy between poets and cats when he says:

> *You a friend of loftier mind*
> *Answer friends alone in kind.*

Matthew Arnold, however, sees the other side of the cat - the 'tearer and render', the side many people find it hard to reconcile with the warm loving cat of the hearth:

> *Cruel, but composed and bland*
> *Dumb, inscrutable and grand*
> *So Tiberius might have sat,*
> *Had Tiberius been a cat.*

My own beautiful little Tiberius was named after this poem. Like his mother Tiny, he would sit for long hours, like an Egyptian statue, 'inscrutable and grand'. His huge aquamarine eyes, set like jewels in his head, added to this impression. I have never seen such remarkable eyes other than in Chinchilla cats: they were exactly the colour that would be obtained if the blue of Tiny's blue eye and the yellow of Tim's, his father's had been paints and skillfully blended by an artist with a sure and certain touch.

On the subject of eyes, probably one of the best- known cat poems is Walter de la Mare's *'Five Eyes'* which is about the three black cats belonging to a miller, one of which had only one eye:

> *Whisker and claw, they crouch in the night,*
> *Their five eyes smouldering. green and bright.*

Like good working cats, they hunt all night till break of day when Hans the miller returns to work; then:

Out come his cats, all grey with meal - Jekkel and Jessup and one-eyed Jill.

Less well-known is another poem by Walter de la Mare, *'As I Mused by the Fireside'*, written in very simple rhyme about a very simple theme - the contentment of sitting by the fire on a cold night with a cat.

> *As I mused by the fireside,*
> *Puss said to me:*
> *There burns the fire, man,*
> *And here sit we.*
> *...Just man and beast met*
> *In this solitude!*
> *Dear God, what security*
> *Comfort and bliss!*
> *And to think too. what ages*
> *Have brought us to this!*

There is something akin in this poem to the rather better-known one by Alexander Gray, *'On A Cat Ageing'*:

He blinks upon the hearth-rug
And yawns in deep content,
Accepting all the comforts
That providence has sent.

And so we come back again to the lion on the mat of chapter one - the cosy cat by the hearth, with talons sheathed; the cat we all love, the representative of home, comfort, warmth and security.

But contrast is the spice of life, and it is probably because we are also keenly aware of the other side of the cat that we can appreciate the home loving side so much.

Ruth Pitter gives us a delightful description of the reverse side in her poem '*Quorum Porum*':

In a dark garden, by a dreadful Tree,
The Druid Toms were met. They numbered Three:
Tab Tiger, Demon Black, and Ginger Hate.
Their forms were tense, Their eyes were full of fate,
Save for the involuntary caudal thrill,
The horror was that they should sit so still.

A familiar sight - and equally familiar are the marrow-freezing yowls that so often follow, as Ruth Pitter goes on to say, 'Like a lost soul that flounders in the murk'.

The kinship between the cat and the moon is a long standing thing, far too deep in antiquity to be denied. The cat is basically nocturnal and her wonderful eyes have the power to utilise to the full any available light. It is particularly hard to keep cats in who want to go out on a moonlit night.

The move to our present home happened to coincide with a full moon. Feeling that Tabitha did not know her bearings sufficiently well at that time to be abroad at night I insisted she stay in. She remained awake most of the night and also ensured I did. The full moon outside the window drew her like a magnet from my bed. She sat behind the curtain gazing out into her new world bathed in pure white light and drank it all in. Unfortunately she could not be content to just do that but had to tell me all about it in her deep, impossible-to-ignore Siamese yowl. Every now and then, just to make sure I was really listening, she jumped on the bed and repeated it all, right in my ear.

Poor Tabitha - she must have felt like Black Minnaloushe in W. B. Yeats' *The Cat and the Moon*:

> *Black Minnaloushe stared at the moon,*
> *For wander and wall as he would,*
> *The pure cold light in the sky*
> *Troubled his animal blood.*

Cats: beautiful, sensuous, cruel, passionate, loving, independent, such a mystery, such a paradox; no wonder so many writers and poets have loved them and mourned for them, as Michael Joseph did in *To a Siamese Cat*:

> *I shall see beauty*
> *But none to match your living grace:*
> *...I shall fill my days.*
> *But I shall not, cannot forget.*

How lucky for us that so many writers and poets love cats - they have given us such a rich feline literature to browse in, and a greater number of cats to know in a lifetime. Cats like Richard Garnett's 'Marigold':

> *She moved through the garden in glory because*
> *She had very long claws at the end of her paws.*
> *Her back was arched, her tall was high,*
> *A green fire glared in her vivid eye.*
> *And all the Toms, though never so bold,*
> *Quailed at the martial Marigold.*

168

I have always had a particularly soft spot for Marigold, though whenever I read this delightful verse it is not an orange-coloured cat that I see in my mind's eye but a small long-haired cat, Fluffy, who looks like a cloud of smoke but who moves in exactly the same way as the martial Marigold - and for the same reasons.

Chapter 13
Cats and Commerce

It took me, I am sorry to say, more than half my life to decide that making money out of animals is just not on - for me anyway. Not only were the feed and veterinary bills always bigger than I expected, but unforeseen disasters and calamities came along that swallowed up any profit there might be in the exercise. Then of course I found it so hard to see my cats as 'pieces of merchandise'; each one was so individual, so much a person.

My first foray into the world of cat shows, when I took Tabitha and her brother Tiger Tim, well and truly whetted my appetite. I was like an actor who had smelled greasepaint! I took Tabitha to all the big cat shows in England and she soon had an impressive list of awards. As soon as she was adult we started off again, this time chasing no mere first prizes but the elusive Challenge Certificates, three of which, won under three different judges, soon earned her the coveted title of Champion.

In Tabitha's first litter by the Red Tabby Champion there was a very pretty Blue-cream kitten. Blue-cream is the dilute form of tortoiseshell, the coat being blue and cream instead of black and red but for some peculiar reason the powers that be in the Cat Fancy decree that whereas in a Tortoiseshell the colours should be distinct and in patches, in the Blue-cream they should be softly mingled. Matilda, my little Blue cream, was really marked more like a Tortie, but she was an exquisite kitten: her head was as round as an apple; her eyes, large and round like her mother's, were the deep brilliant amber of her aristocratic father. Her breeding, with nothing but tabby behind her, was totally wrong for a Blue-cream, for any barring on the coat is a fault in either blue or cream varieties. She should really have been spayed and sold as a pet but she was bought by a breeder of British Shorthair cats who wanted to breed a variety of colours. I have no doubt she succeeded, for Matilda had just about every colour in her ancestry!

I thought she was beautiful, and showing had me in its spell, so I asked her new owner if I could keep her for a few weeks and take her to the Bristol Show.

By this time I was really doing things in style. My cats no longer travelled in the wicker travelling hamper but in a specially designed case made by the husband of a fellow cat breeder. These cases were designed to look like ordinary suitcases but a flap on what appeared to be the lid let down and revealed two compartments with wire doors. The main idea behind the design, it must be confessed, was to deceive railway and hotel officials as to the contents of the case! Nevertheless they were also very comfortable for the cats, for they were able to stand upright and stretch as well as curl up in comfort. It was, however, rather important to have the weight reasonably balanced in each side, otherwise the inmates would be sitting on an uncomfortable slope when it was being carried. It was even more important to keep both a firm eye and hand on the case otherwise some overenthusiastic hotel or railway porter (this was in the days when one did get one's cases carried!) was more than likely to swing it onto a rack and place it on its side - not good for the inmates!

I decided to take not only Tabitha and Matilda to the Bristol Show but Blanche as well. Blanche was Tiny's daughter, the one who had been sold and brought back because she was too expensive for their child to maul.

By the time I set off I was well loaded with cat-carrying case. A case with my own overnight things and another (larger) bag with the cat's necessities: show blankets, feeding bowls, grooming gear, food, sanitary tray and a large supply of newspaper which I had found from experience to be the best material for the tray when travelling. We travelled first class as I had made the curious discovery that with a first-class ticket I was seldom asked what was in the case, or why I didn't put it on the rack. It was simply accepted that I wanted to keep my large suitcase standing upright on the floor by me, and in first-class compartments there was always room to do this.

The case was such a good imitation of an ordinary suitcase that it was very amusing sometimes when one of the cats, usually the vocal Tabitha, miaowed, to see people looking around trying to locate the source of the sound. They very seldom made any comment - no doubt only half-believing they had heard it!

On one memorable occasion I was with the friend whose husband had made the cases. She had a similar one containing her beautiful Silver Tabby cats. We were leaving a large London show hall in search of a taxi. To be strictly accurate we were being chased by an irate cat lover brandishing an umbrella and threatening to call the police and report us to RSPCA and anybody else who might listen. We were secretly quite relieved to flag down a cruising cab almost at once and direct him to drive, with all speed, to Euston Station. In actual fact the cats were probably more comfortable in their case than in a conventional basket, and they certainly had ample air.

I had discovered that travelling with my cat case first class was not only more comfortable but sound economics, for no-one questioned the contents of the case and I never bothered to buy tickets for them. (British Rail in those days both accepted cats as travellers and charged for them!).

Having arrived in Bristol I made my way to the large and comfortable hotel that I had booked into fairly near the show hall and, trying to look as nonchalant and blasé as possible, checked in and followed the hall porter, who was carrying my case, to the lift. To my relief the cats kept quiet. British hotels, like the railways, charge for cats - if they accept them!

Alone in the room I let the cats out, filled the tray with newspaper and their feed bowls with the lean minced beef I had brought with me, and went down to dine myself.

When I returned Tabitha and Matilda were curled up together in the middle of the bed. There was no sign of Blanche. I had searched, quite frantically in every likely and unlikely spot in the room, 'helped' by Tabitha and Matilda, before I heard a small miaow from somewhere way above my head. I looked up but it was some time before I saw the gleeful Cheshire grin surrounded by white fur and topped by two sparkling kitten eyes looking at me over the pelmet of the heavy chenille curtains that draped the huge window in the high-ceilinged Victorian room. It was quite impossible to reach her, a fact which she knew quite as well as I did!

'Blanche!' I commanded, 'come down at once!' I should of course have known better than to assume such a tone with a cat, especially Tiny's daughter.

Blanche shouted back at me something like, 'shan't!' or maybe 'can't', or perhaps it was, 'come and get me if you want me!' Her eyes glittered with mischief as she swung round, not to come down but to proceed crabwise across the pelmet until she was in exactly the same position on the other side

She was apparently rather pleased with this performance, because however much I begged, bossed, cajoled and entreated, this was all she would do, back and forth across that wretched pelmet far above my head. At last, quite exhausted, I did what I should have done in the first place - ignored her. I undressed and went to bed, with the other two securely locked in the cat case!

The light was out and I was just dropping off into a weary sleep when I heard the sound of claws on cloth followed by a soft thud as she landed on the carpet. A few seconds later there was another, softer but closer thud as she jumped on the bed, a small cold nose was pressed against my cheek, a purr hummed near my ear and Blanche and I dropped to sleep.

I woke bright and early, but not so early as Blanche, who was grinning down at me from her perch on the pelmet!

Why on earth hadn't I roused myself sufficiently to put her in the travelling case when I had the chance? I imagined us all spending the day locked in the hotel bedroom and never getting to the show at all! I needn't have worried: breakfast brought her down. I made sure she ate it secure in the travelling case!

Cat showing is a relatively pleasant and easy business, for both cats and owners, compared with other forms of livestock exhibition. All the cats have to do is sit in a pen and be pleasant to judges and stewards when the moment for judging comes: the owners are not required, or even allowed, to be present. I spent an enjoyable morning exploring Bristol, a city I had never visited before, and returned after lunch to see how my trio had acquitted themselves.

Tabitha had the usual good showing of prize cards I had come to expect of her; Matilda had won-two firsts, a second and a third. Blanche had two seconds, a third, a Very Highly Commended and a special card on her pen. As she peered out from behind her cards there seemed to be an amused glint in her eye. I looked in her pen where the special prize had been placed. A tin of flea powder! Flea powder for my pristine pure little white kitten who had been bathed in the best shampoo (for humans) before she left home. I hastily removed it and tucked it in my bag lest the admiring public should think she really needed it!

But Blanche's day had not finished: a photographer was at the show taking photos for *The Observer's Book of Cats* and he picked Blanche to represent the British whites: her day at a show was not to be forgotten!

This was a period in my life when I was probably learning more about cats than at any other time. I was involved with them from every angle. I was breeding them, showing them, boarding them and writing about them, and all the time I was learning!

Boarding cats seemed such an easy thing when I first hit on the idea, and my father gave me the use of an old cottage on the property. It was a tiny little two-up and two-down cottage with twisty wooden stairs and sloping ceilings in the bedrooms. The two downstairs rooms were dank and cold, getting no sun, but the upstairs rooms whose windows faced the sun were quite different. I used the smaller one as a store room for sawdust, tins of cat food, etc., and the larger one as a cattery. I had six pens built in: four single ones and two large double ones for cats from the same home.

Each pen was painted in cream gloss paint; the floor covered with adhesive red plastic, and was furnished with a little wicker basket with a blue blanket, a sanitary tray and a ping-pong ball. These were much appreciated by even quite sedate cats and often I would open the door downstairs and hear the noise of several balls being batted around simultaneously.

It was pleasant, quiet and cosy in my cattery. It was sunny in summer and I had installed an electrical wall heater beaming on the pens for winter. The only labour required was a twice-daily visit to change trays and dispense food. I had bookings stretching ahead through the summer months at 3 shillings a day per cat, quite a reasonable sum of money in those days. I had forgotten that cats were individuals, personalities - hotel guests, not inanimate things.

There was the 'dear' little Siamese who came for a fortnight. For the entire time I had to wear thick leather gauntlets to handle her; she would even attack the hand that placed the food bowl in her pen, and getting her tray out to change was a work of art. Came the end of the fourteen days and the return of her owners, she shouted with joy on seeing them, stepped out of her pen, smiled up into my face and rubbed round my legs. Her owners were most impressed as they thought we had been on such good terms all along!

There were the cats who sat crouched in bed, or worse still huddled in the corner behind the bed, eyes wide and fearful, totally immobile and refusing all food. I learned that talking to them and coaxing was not the thing to do. I merely alarmed them more. Eventually they would unfreeze and eat if I just put the food in the pen and ignored them.

The window, which of course was an upstairs one, was wired up for safety and visitors who had settled in were often let out into the room where they could sit on the window-sill in the sun, admire the view or just 'talk' to other residents. This seemed an excellent arrangement - until Jasper came to stay, all the way from Salisbury in the south of England.

He was sent to me by train by his owner Vere Temple, the well-known artist and writer, because he was a 'special' cat; she was going away and didn't want to leave him to the care of the~ person who was coming in daily to feed her other cats.

He was a massive and splendidly handsome un-neutered male cat, a shorthair Brown Tabby. Vere Temple adored him - and he her, as subsequent events proved.

All went well till the last few days of his stay, when I went into the cattery one evening at feed time to find the wire torn away from the window and no Jasper!

Love, they say, laughs at locksmiths. Jasper must have laughed at my wire netting as he ripped it away to answer the call of a neighbours in-season female cat!

Frantically we searched and called far into the night; our torches occasionally picked up the gleam of eyes, but we did not catch him. This continued for two days and nights. Always the brief sightings, the sound of his voice somewhere. Never the chance to catch him or even get reasonably near. Finally I sent a telegram to Vere Temple.

The time was fast approaching when I should be despatching him back home by rail, and she was not on the phone. She got to one, however, the minute she received my wire and informed me, tersely, that she would be on the next train, which was due to arrive at our local station around teatime and would I meet her?

I mobilised all the help available and redoubled, if that were possible, the efforts to capture him. How wonderful it would be if I could announce that he was once more safely under lock and key when we met!

Alas, I had no such good news to report and my meeting with Vere Temple was difficult, to say the least. Though I admired her restraint, I very much doubt if in the same circumstances I would have been so restrained.

Back home I offered her tea. She said very firmly that she could not possibly eat or drink a thing until she had Jasper! 'Dear God!' I thought, 'she'll starve to death!' But she was quite adamant.

She asked which area he had last been seen in. I informed her that he had not been seen at all but I thought I had heard him in the garden. She instructed us all to keep out of her way and remain silent. She started at the front in the rose garden, working her way through the flower beds towards the vegetables. As she walked down the pathway between the two long herbaceous borders, speaking rather than calling his name, a wonderful sight met my eyes.

Out from the thick cover of the delphinium plants calmly strolled a large and magnificent tabby cat; he answered her voice with a deep guttural yowl of greeting and threw himself down at her feet where he rolled about in ecstasy. She bent down and scooped him up in her arms. It had taken her no more than five minutes to find and recapture him - though recapture seems hardly the right word for such a joyful reunion.

We all went in for tea, and there being no trains back to Salisbury that night she stayed with us - with Jasper sleeping in her room.

Vere Temple proved to be a most charming and gracious lady in the very best sense of the words. She refused my offer to reimburse her train fare and only with difficulty did I persuade her to at least let me waive Jasper's hotel bill. She inspected my cattery and pointed out to me the total inadequacies of my 'cat escape-proofing' against such large, powerful and determined cats as Jasper.

A year later Jasper was killed in an accident. Vere Temple bought a brown tabby son of Tabitha and Tiberius (Tim), Tiny's son. This kitten could never replace Jasper - no cat could do that - but he did grow into a handsome and loving cat. She also had previously bought Colette, one of Tiny's white daughters. She and I only met personally once more, at a cat show in London, but over the years we kept up quite a correspondence.

After Jasper's visit I had my cat proofing redone and also decided in future not to accept un-neutered male cats as boarders. However strong the wire, I decided the call of sex might well prove stronger. I could not expect another escapee or its owner to be of the calibre of Jasper and Vere Temple!

In spite of escapees, difficult cats (and owners) and one terrible time when a wave of cat flu swept through the inmates and I had to close down in the middle of the peak summer season until the cattery itself was safe from infection, I enjoyed boarding cats. I also learned a great deal about cat nature. Many of my 'regulars' settled in as if they had never been away, even if they only came for one visit a year, remembering exactly when meals were served, proving that the cat's memory is quite as good as ours.

I saw so many happy reunions with cats and owners that I would never again say that cats were not affectionate. I also met many delightful people during this period. Even over the cat flu episode, the only person who was annoyed and unpleasant about their cat being sick while on holiday was the owner of the cat who brought in the infection!

During this period in my life there seemed to be cats everywhere. The attics of our large old house were utilised as a kitten creche; from down below the sound of umpteen little kitten feet running around made it sound as if we were overrun with rats! In fact my father, seeing people in his office, often had to explain the noise to them.

When they got older I had a large wire run outside where they could play in safety out of harm and mischief until they were old enough either to go to their new homes or be promoted to full freedom.

If sometimes I seemed to be quite overrun with cats then I only had to visit some of my friends to reassure me that I had a long way to go! Gladys lived near Birmingham in a large rambling country house and garden with no less than sixty cats of assorted sizes and colours.

Showing was my hobby and relaxation in those days. I was an unashamed 'pot-hunter' with a cat like Tabitha, who loved every minute of it and always won plenty of prizes, it was really both a pleasure and a relaxation, but certainly not, as I realised when I totted up my large expenses and infinitesimal returns, a profitable occupation!

Tiny did not go on these excursions; odd-eyed whites are not generally considered show cats, however beautiful they may be in the eyes of their doting owners! Also, she never had a good coat. I have no means of knowing but I always felt this was probably yet another inheritance of her dreadful kittenhood and the time when she lost all her hair. It was always of a rather coarse texture and a little too long for a shorthaired cat. Since all her kittens had beautiful thick, plush coats of the type so desired by breeders of British Shorthairs I felt this poor coat must have been caused, rather than inherited.

When we returned from shows she greeted both me and her friend Tabitha, and even her daughters and sons, with a chilly hauteur. It usually took at least half an hour or so, during which she stayed with me, watching me unpack and generally settle back in before she would allow me to pick her up. Then her little arms would tighten around my neck, sometimes with the thumb claw just sticking in, she would purr - and I knew I was forgiven!

If I had been out anywhere else, without the other cats, it was quite different: I was welcomed home immediately I got back. She would greet me with little shouts and 'prrt!'s of joy, and when I picked her up the arms would tighten round my neck and the happy purr thrum in my ear.

It wasn't always purring I heard in my ear though; when I fetched her in to bed from a dusky garden on a summer evening, for instance, I would hear angry growls throbbing menacingly in my ear. She would be rigid in my arms and all claws would be unsheathed and sticking into the back of my neck, her tail twitching and her eyes flashing angry messages at me.

It was on one of these occasions that we came to blows - the only time in the ten years we were together. I was going out, and as I usually did on such occasions, I went out to the garden to bring her in to the safety of my room. She was prowling about down at the far end of the vegetable garden, totally ignoring my calls. I had an appointment and time was growing short. I hurried down the garden and swept her up. She swung into the inevitable position with her right arm round my neck, all the claws sticking in; her eyes were flashing ominously and she was growling in a high-pitched menacing voice telling me she did not want to leave whatever she was doing and come in. I was angry too, and for a brief second we glared at one another. Then, swift and sure, she struck my nose with her left paw, also with all claws unsheathed. The sudden sharp pain brought the tears to my eyes; angrily I retaliated by hitting her sharply on the nose with my forefinger. She sneezed but kept her paw raised and her eyes flashing into mine.

For what seemed a long time we remained like that, each with a hand poised to strike, each glaring at the other, me very conscious of the sting where she had scratched me and the blood slowly trickling down my face. Then I felt the arm round my neck relax, ever so slightly, and the upraised paw slowly went down. Tiny conceded defeat and we never, either of us, ever struck the other again.

This was a period in my life when I had so many cats I was almost losing count. As if that wasn't enough, I had my boarders in the cattery and I was trundling round England to every possible cat show. It was at one of these shows that I bought Teddy.

Teddy wasn't his real name, but we called him that because he was such a big cuddly cat - with people. His pedigree name was 'Killlnghall Red Spark' and he was a young Red Tabby stud cat.

A pedigree Red Tabby is quite different from an ordinary ginger moggy. It is red, the colour of a red setter being the ideal.

He was a magnificent cat, with huge deep amber eyes and a rich red coat with tabby markings in a lighter shade: but what a character! With people he was the softest cuddliest 'sook' imaginable, who more than lived up to his pet name.

With other cats however, he was not just a spark but a ball of fire: a wolf with females, with other males a tiger. Dogs he treated as if they didn't exist.

He lived in a cat house for some twenty or twenty-two hours out of the twenty-four because two or three hours was about the limit anyone could stand him free and on the rampage.

The minute I let him out in the morning he would race off, yowling to the world at large that he was coming, hell-bent on raping any female cat he met and killing any male cat. Poor old Gussie, for some extraordinary reason (she had been spayed for some time by now), was the object of his attention.

He had only to catch a glimpse in the distance of white fur and he was off. The second she saw him, Gussie was off too, with Teddy in hot pursuit. She usually headed for the house and having reached its sanctuary would complain bitterly to us that he never even gave her time to tell him about her operation!

Teddy was never any trouble to get back in again: after a couple of hours of chasing, raping and fighting he would head for the house, drop down exhausted on the cool tiles of the kitchen floor and lie there, panting like a dog. I would give him liquid refreshment, scoop him up and shut him up, and everyone breathed a big sigh of relief until next morning.

Teddy

I kept him four months, during which time I mated him to Tabitha, her Blue tabby daughter, Silky, and to a visiting tortoiseshell; then I sold him to my friend near Birmingham with sixty cats. Enough to keep even Teddy happy! I had learned a valuable lesson - keeping a stud cat was not the easy way of making money I had previously imagined!

I wasn't quite through with him though even after he left. Twenty-four hours later the phone rang.

'You must come over!' Gladys begged. 'Teddy has got out - he's fighting the tomcat from up the road. I'm sure he'll be killed!'

I expressed my doubts on that score.

'But he might not come in!' she walled. 'He knows you better than me, he'd come for you.'

'He'll come,' I assured her, 'when he's ready!' I could tell she didn't believe me, but I managed to persuade her to have one last try before I set out on the thirty mile drive to her home.

A few minutes later she was back on the phone; Teddy had returned through the fence, bloody but triumphant, and thrown himself down, panting, at her feet!

I soon had kittens everywhere. Tiny had three kittens by a champion British Blue cat, Tabitha had three by Teddy and Silky her daughter had six by him. Twelve kittens to sell; but fate had a sharp lesson in store for me.

One by one Silky's kittens faded out. There was no other way to describe it. For no apparent reason, they died. They did not have cleft palates or anything visibly wrong with them. The vet was as mystified as I was. Finally a month after they were born I only had one left, a beautiful little red female called Marigold. Then she began to sneeze - she had cat flu. Silky, never a devoted mother, abandoned her at once and I was left with the task of feeding her with an eye dropper and trying to cure her of cat flu. I did not succeed. I had lost the entire litter and what was worse, Tiny's beautiful kittens, just ready to go to their new homes, were sneezing. I saved them all, but it was another two months before they were fit to leave home. By a system of rigorous isolation I managed to prevent the infection spreading to Tabitha's family. These were a blue tabby male who was neutered and sold as a pet and two Tortoiseshell females, Peggy Sue and Patty, both of whom went to breeders, had distinguished show careers and became champions.

Tortoiseshells - torties for short - are fascinating cats. One would imagine that tortie is the same colour as tortie-and-white, minus the white patches. Not so. Tortie-and-white cats are a blend of black and red with white markings. They are born the colour they will be at maturity. Torties on the other hand, are a mixture of black, red and cream. This in itself is odd, as cream is a dilute form of red, and it would not seem possible to have the dilute and normal form of a colour in the same cat. Torties are born nearly black with only faint bits of red or cream showing. The colours come through as the kitten grows; one born looking a good colour will end up far too red. This colouring is one of the few cases of sex-linking in mammals. Torties and tortie and whites are always female.

By the time I had sold six kittens, not twelve, and had paid off my vet's bills and totted up the extra feed bills for Tiny's kittens, who had to stay with me (with steadily growing appetites) two months longer than anticipated, I was well out of pocket. Breeding kittens was not a good money-making exercise either!

After Silky's lamentable performance as a mother she was spayed and sold to a good home. I decided in future to go in for quality not quantity, and to try to keep my cat family down to reasonable proportions so that I could enjoy them to the full.

I was learning - but I had a long way to go yet!

Chapter 14
A Comedy of Cats

The idea of there being anything funny about cats seems to strike some people as almost sacrilegious. Cats are beautiful, stately, haughty; dignified, even selfish - but funny? No! They may concede that kittens can be entertaining to watch, but once they reach maturity all that frivolity goes and they must be respected.

Cats, I maintain, are exactly like people. Some are serious, even stately, most are thoroughly selfish (if you call looking after Number One selfish), some are haughty, most like to be dignified and some are funny. What is more, they seem to enjoy being funny.

Tabitha the first was a glorious comedienne who loved nothing more than playing to the gallery; The time I found her at the show eating her meat with her paw to the admiration and applause of the crowd she was wallowing in every sound of appreciation and obviously thought that my untimely return would spoil the fun.

Honey, my Abyssinian was another natural comedienne. For a few years there was a lull in my cat activities: after Tabitha was spayed and had gone to a new home because of her refusal to come to terms with my mother's boxer bitch, I had Tim (Tiberius, son of Tiny) neutered. Tiny was already spayed. This left me with no breeding cats. I had itchy feet; the big wide world beckoned and like Dick Whittington I set off with only my cat, Tiny, for company.

Honey

Over the next few years I lived in flats in Oxford and London trying to make a living as a freelance journalist and taking jobs when I couldn't. Then I married and went to live on a farm in Bedfordshire. Tiny came too of course.

When Graham, my eldest son, was eight months old, the lure of the show world beckoned. I had not quite got it out of my system! I bought a female Abyssinian kitten; her pedigree name was Shybu Aurnm, but in the family she was known as Honey. I soon discovered that I had brought another Tabitha into the family!

Honey was like half-a-dozen cats all rolled into one. She had prodigious energy; a huge appetite, a love of people and a quite zany sense of humour. Graham loved her and she him.

We were then living in a huge English farmhouse built in Victorian times. It had high ceilings with tall windows, and a wide staircase coming down from the landing above to a tiled hallway below. Two of Honey's favourite games were shinning wildly up the kitchen curtains after a flying leap over my pot-plants on the wide sill below, and shouting in gleeful Abyssinian from the top. This performance was guaranteed to make Graham in his high chair shout with laughter and bang his spoon appreciatively on the tray, which in turn encouraged Honey in even wilder exploits. Down she would come, zip round the kitchen and then up the other curtain where she would turn round and look directly at Graham waiting for the next round of applause and encouragement.

Another game she loved was retrieving a ball of paper. I have only had two cats in my life do this, the first Tabitha and Honey. Honey liked to play this game on the stairs, with me on the landing. I would throw a twist of paper over the banisters to the hall below; she would watch it drop, then race along the landing, round the corner and down the stairs, but hallway she would jump through the banisters to the hall below, pick up the paper in her teeth, race for the stairs, often skidding on the tiles as she turned the corner, gallop up and drop the paper at my feet for a repeat performance.

She kept Graham happy and amused for hours. When he was out in the garden in his pram she would jump in with him and play with him. When they both tired they would drop to sleep together, Honey always at his feet, never around his face. On the rare occasions she jumped down out of the pram while he was still awake, I would hear the most heartbroken walls coming from the deserted Graham.

With only six months difference in their ages they seemed to understand one another perfectly, I never remember Graham hurting Honey, or Honey scratching Graham.

One thing Honey did however did not amuse Graham. She had more than a large appetite and was prepared to sample anything. She would sit on the back of Graham's high chair, or rather, perch there, and when she saw a tasty-looking morsel on its way to his mouth would reach one incredibly long arm over his shoulder, neatly hook the tit-bit off his spoon and transfer it to her own mouth.

This was a wonderful appetite sharpener and I never had any trouble persuading Graham to eat up his meals!

Like Tabitha she used her paws a great deal. I soon learned to banish her from the kitchen when I was baking, as she would leap onto the table and dip a paw into my cake mixture to 'try' it before my very eyes! She never had any sense of guilt. 'What's yours is mine!' was her philosophy.

One day I had visitors coming for afternoon tea and in the morning I baked, and rolled successfully, a Swiss roll. I had just placed it on the cooling rack, with some pride, when the phone went. Hurrying to answer it, I left the kitchen door a cat-crevice open. When I returned Honey was happily munching through my perfect Swiss roll - from both ends! I spent most of the rest of the day furiously baking before my visitors arrived because of course the next roll - and the next - resolutely refused to roll.

Honey's greed did have one advantage however. She simply could not resist beaten raw egg. I sometimes gave her an egg, which I would beat in a bowl with a fork, and the sound of a fork being knocked around a bowl was absolutely guaranteed to bring her in so long as she was within hearing distance.

Of course now I had a show cat again I could not resist showing, and living within seventy miles of the London shows it was possible for me to get to a show without staying the night away from home. One show morning Honey managed to elude me and slip out into the garden. Frantically I called and searched while the time for the early morning train to London grew inexorably nearer. At last I did what I should have done in the first place, just stood at the back door banging a fork around in a bowl. Out from the fruit bushes just near the door strolled Honey, tail a wave, beaming expectantly; she had been watching me look for her all the time!

I waited till she was safely through the door before I made a grab and flung her into the travelling box. We just made the train!

She had a gold collar and lead which looked 'tres chic' on her tawny tabby coat; she seemed to think so too and never minded wearing it. Once on the train I would let her out of her travelling box and, with the lead on for security, she would stand on the seat, paws on the window ledge, looking out of the window for the sixty-odd-mile train journey into London.

She enjoyed shows themselves almost as much as Tabitha had done, so showing her was pleasurable rather than tiresome, and I enjoyed my return to the show world, renewing old friendships and making new ones.

Abyssinians, like most other 'foreign' breeds of cat, have rather long hind legs which gives them a graceful, swaying walk. I sometimes thought Honey accentuated this when she wanted to impress!

I was standing at the back door talking to a young man who had come to see John on business one day when Honey strolled in past us. As she walked between us she looked up and gave a gracious yowl, then calmly sat down and looked at us. The young man watched her enthralled, the sales spiel he had been giving me cut out like a switched-off radio.

'What sort of cat is that?' he asked when he found his voice. I told him that she was an Abyssinian, adding, sales spiel for sales spiel, 'They are supposed to be the direct descendants of the sacred cats of Ancient Egypt.'

He was gazing at her as if he had never seen a cat before.

'She's beautiful!' he breathed. 'I've never seen anything like her ... that walk!'

This of course was the cue for Honey to get up and stroll past us, swaying her hips in her mannequin's walk. It became a set performance and quite often drew admiration - though never quite as much as that first time.

My two Tabithas and Honey all had something very much in common - a kind of swaggering joie de vivre, an unquenchable belief in their own worth. A contagious belief - I adored them all!

I remember the first Tabitha being missing once when suppertime came. As she always took great care of the inner cat this was cause for concern. I hunted and called, but there was not a sign of her. I finally heard muffled yowls coming from a pile of junk in a corner of the attic. I still could not find her, but at last following the sound I located her, stuck head fast down a cardboard tube that was almost perpendicular. I put my hand down and was able to reach her tail and pull her up backwards.

She was extremely relieved. It must have been frightening and claustrophobic down there. 'Tabitha!' I said, 'When will you learn? Curiosity could, and very nearly did, kill this cat!'

A sense of humour is probably a necessary part of the survival kit required to live with a cat successfully, though it must be confessed that our sense of humour about cats is often at the cat's expense. We see it as humourous when Puss is brought down a peg or two, her dignity ruffled: banana-skin humour.

It is not easy to appreciate the situation when your cat swaggers into the lounge when you are enjoying after-dinner coffee with an austere great-aunt (from whom one has expectations) and announces that he has killed the furry monster that has taken over your bed, and to prove it he has brought a piece to show you. This really happened to friends of mine who early in their marriage shared their small flat with a truly diabolical black monster called appropriately enough, Satan.

My friend told me that she would never forget the cold horror when she bent down to receive the 'gift' and recognised it as a piece of her husband's aunt's mink stole!

The unsolicited gift from a cat of a dead animal or bird is probably one of the greatest honours it can bestow, but one that is sometimes a little hard to accept graciously, especially when it is a dead rat placed across your foot in the darkness of the pantry, as Muggins did to my mother one day, or a neighbour's duckling on the pillow by your face one Sunday morning, as happened to another friend when she was having a peaceful lie-in. The giver of this particular gift was Sinall, a little black cat who on another occasion climbed up an Indian hawker to sit on his turban as he sheltered from a storm.

If much of our humour at the cat's expense lies in seeing her lose a little of her precious dignity; it must also be admitted that the cat's humour at our expense would seem to lie in putting us in a difficult or embarrassing situation.

My mother recently had a stray ginger cat which she was giving breakfast every morning. It was both very thin and very nervous and she was somewhat annoyed to see the Siamese cat from across the road coming over and eating his breakfast. She was unable to stop it because while the ginger stray was terrified of people the Siamese was not in the least, so the minute she put in an appearance to send the Siamese off the poor ginger just bolted and left the intruder a clear field.

Mother was most indignant when the person owned by the Siamese charged across the road one morning, swept her darling up in her arms and soundly attacked my mother for feeding. it, adding that she had already had to take it to the vet because it was too fat! Mother was most annoyed that she had not gone into the attack first and complained about the Siamese coming over and stealing the food intended for the hungry stray. When she told me the story Mother added that she was quite sure the damned cat was thoroughly enjoying it all!

It does seem at times as if our cats really enjoy embarrassing us. I remember once going to an excellent production of one of Noel Coward's plays while staying at the seaside resort of LLandudno in north Wales.

We had just taken our seats when the theatre cat, a handsome black shorthair, appeared and rubbed around our legs. He chose us because since my mother always carried punctuality to extremes we were the first people in the theatre.

Halfway through the production he successfully stopped the action by walking sedately onto centre stage, up to the leading man and rubbing around his legs. For a moment the entire cast froze and looked at the cat, who then sat down calmly and began to wash. The leading man was the first to pull himself together. 'Just a minute,' he said, clearly, 'I'll have to put the cat out!' He picked it up, walked calmly to the wings and handed it to a waiting hand, returned to centre stage and continued with his role as written.

As anyone knows, if the cat had been required to walk on stage, actually getting it on - on cue - would be the most difficult thing in the world; which probably explains why although dogs often take stage roles, cats very seldom do.

The early days of cat showing must have given the cats themselves ample scope for their peculiar talents, for it was quite common for the neuter cats, or cats of no sex' as they were discreetly described in the catalogues of Victorian and Edwardian shows, to be exhibited not in pens but on leashes. The practice was very quickly abandoned for cats of very definite male sex for obvious reasons!

It does not take a great deal of imagination to visualise the havoc that some ten to twenty cats all on leads could create if they so desired; in my experience the leash on a cat is a mere safety line to prevent it escaping altogether but by no means the control that it is on a dog.

Cat shows, even modern ones, provide a wonderful chance to study people, they are in themselves. a comedy of cats, though I am sure most owners and breeders would be most indignant at such a suggestion!

The first thing that inevitably strikes one on entering a cat show is the noise coming from the Siamese section. There is no doubt about it, they are the garrulous extroverts of the cat world. Having accustomed ones' ears to this, second thing to notice is that so many cats and their owners are so remarkably alike!

194

I don't mean that the Siamese people are all shouting their heads off, (though they do have to talk rather loudly to make themselves heard at all), but they tend to be - sophisticated, well-groomed, eloquent. Moving through the hall to the Persian exhibits one detects a different atmosphere: here dignity is what matters - gracious, well-bred dignity, and more than a hint of cool superiority.

The question of people being like their animals - inevitably poses the question: do they choose animals which are like themselves or do they grow like them? Yet another permutation of the age-old riddle 'which came first - the chicken or the egg?'

The Persians do not usually complain vocally like the Siamese, nor do they hold lengthy conversations with perfect strangers. They maintain an aloof dignity, if they condescend to notice where they are at all. As often as not they retreat into some secret inner place - perhaps the astral plane.

How often at a cat show have I wished that I could really get inside the mind of just one of the participants and see the whole proceedings from his or her point of view. Somehow I have an uncomfortable feeling that I might find the tables turned and that instead of cats on view for people it was people on parade to be studied by cats; and we just might not look so good!

The great cat joke is of course getting stuck up a tree. Or rather, pretending to be stuck up a tree. A friend of mine was once well and truly taken in by this one.

Mary lived in the London suburb of Hampstead and bred beautiful British Blue-and-Silver Tabby cats. One of her young British Blues shinned up the tallest of tall trees in her front garden one day and then proceeded to tell the world she was stuck! No amount of coaxing and calling would bring her own. In desperation Mary called the RSPCA, who in turn told her to call the fire brigade. This she did, and much to her relief they came with their tall ladders and rescued the marooned kitten.

The cat, she told me afterwards, appeared to enjoy every minute of the proceedings and the attention and admiration she received when finally rescued. Imagine Mary's horror when she did the same thing next day! This time she determined to harden her heart and leave her there; but when she was still there the next meal time she once more phoned the fire brigade. As they parked beneath the tree and started organising their gear, down the tree at the double came the cat to rub around their ankles, purring happily when she reached terra firma! My poor friend had never felt so embarrassed in her life. She apologised obsequiously to the firemen and told that cat, in no uncertain terms, that she would never, ever, no matter what, do anything to rescue her if she ever got stuck up a tree again!

Curiously enough over the many years that I have lived with cats there have been two cats, and two only, who have fallen into the bath with me! The curious thing is that they were the two Tabithas. And both were doing the same thing, walking around the rim of the bath, showing off, and holding a conversation with me that went something along the lines of 'Hey, look at me, aren't I clever?'

I must confess I laughed heartily when with a pained look at me, they pulled themselves up out of the water. But Tabitha Two had the last laugh when she did it; she sat on my dry clothes to lick herself dry!

I used to find dear old Gussie an entertaining sight in the long twilight of English summer evenings. She delighted in hunting moths on the tennis court! From the landing windows of the house I had a grandstand view of what appeared to be a small phantom player leaping about after an invisible ball as the white cat jumped about on her hind legs batting away with her front paws.

Ruth has a young cat, Kit, who appears to have a pronounced sense of humour. Ruth had gone to fetch the mail one day and as Kit had followed her to the box on the road she picked her up. A young cyclist passing by stopped to ask his way. Just as Ruth directed him, Kit reached up, caught the brim of her peaked sun cap in her paw and pulled it down over Ruth's face!

Cats love being laughed with when they are putting on a performance specially for our benefit, and they also thoroughly enjoy laughing at us, but they absolutely hate us to laugh at them. When we forget ourselves and do this, as even the most controlled of us must do at times, they will immediately seek to regain lost face by totally ignoring us and indulging in a very thorough wash.

How often must we cat devotees wish that we could do the same when our tiresome charges make us lose face?

Chapter 15
Cat Conversations

I was quite horrified when I once heard people say that they thought they would have to have their cat put down because she talked too much! She is a spayed female so her 'talking' is all along conversational lines; they do not have to put up with the 'calling' of an in-season queen and the banshee shrieks of attendant lovers, or would-be lovers.

To me, one of the most delightful attributes of my cats is the way they talk to me, and back at me when I talk to them. Obviously such cat conversations are not to everyone's taste: a friend of mine has a beautiful Siamese who was given to her some years ago because his owner objected to being talked at by a cat. She threw cushions at him to shut him up. Of course that didn't work. He simply shinned up the curtains and instead of just talking hurled abuse at her. He too, would have been silenced for ever if Jill hadn't given him a home. Siamese are renowned for their voices, so it seems the height of absurdity in the first place to buy one if you don't like the idea of being talked to by a cat.

I think that one of Tabitha's most delightful qualities is her voice. Half-Siamese (strictly speaking one-quarter Siamese, for her mother is a Tonkinese, that is, a Siamese- Burmese cross), Tabitha has the deep throaty voice associated with Siamese cats.

When she greets me the noise she makes is the nearest thing to 'hello' I have ever heard an animal make. In fact it would not take a very big jump of the imagination to believe that she is saying 'hello' and that I have a talking cat on my hands!

Admittedly there have been times when I have found her conversation a little tiring: when we first moved into our present home for instance and she insisted on looking out into the moonlight and telling me, in a very loud voice, what she saw out there - at two in the morning: but on the whole I find her vocal qualities a sheer delight.

Siamese, of course, are not by any means the only cats who 'talk'; most cats do, but having more modest and moderate voices we probably don't notice them so much.

Many white cats are very vocal, particularly those with the deafness associated with blue eyes. They often have loud and rather inane voices, because they cannot hear what they are saying!

Perhaps it is because of this affliction running through them that all white cats tend to talk a lot. Sheba has a wonderful vocabulary and can run through an incredible range of miaows when she wants out, or in, or something to eat, or a drink of milk or just attention. A range that starts at the 'Poor little me!' end of the scale and ends at 'Do as I say!' at the other.

The miaow is of course not the sum total of the cat's vocal range, and in this I include the yowl. Cats also purr - that unique song of sheer contentment sung only by felines - and they growl. The growl of an angry cat can be every bit as menacing as that of a dog, and certainly seems to have a greater range from a deep, deep rumble to quite a horrible high-pitched note just before the growl turns into a yowl!

There is also the soft little 'prrt!' of affection, something like a very short burst of purr. This is the sound reserved by the mother cat to greet her kittens, and by all cats to greet their people - which seems to put owners somewhere in the same category as kittens! For all that, it is a sound that is truly music to the ear of the doting cat person!

Cats, like every other creature including humans, use a lot of non-vocal language in their communication with both their own and other species. Like us they use their eyes to flash with anger; the pupils will widen with fear, the eyes themselves distending to round orbs; while the sleepy happy, or just plain contented cat will have eyes that are mere oriental slits.

Cats use their eyes to throw kisses too. when your cat looks into your face, purrs happily, and slowly and very deliberately closes both eyes in a blink or two eyed wink, it is saying, 'I love you,' and throwing you a kiss. You can throw one back. Most exciting of all you can be the first to throw a kiss. Cats being what they are, don't always expect a response; but what a thrill when the cat kisses back. Sometimes you may meet a strange cat sunning itself on a wall or something. If it is in a benevolent mood it may well answer the kiss thrown to it by returning the compliment.

Cats also possess something we do not that is a great aid to communication - a tail. At least most cats do. Manx cats, who do not, often chatter in a peculiar way when excited or angry as a compensation for having no tail to twitch or wave.

The aggressive or startled cat will fluff her tail up to twice its normal size, the angry cat will swish it about, and the happy cat welcoming you home will carry its tail stiff and perpendicular, an obelisk of greeting.

If we take the time to watch and observe our cats and to really listen to them when they are being vocal we will find that we understand a great deal of what they are saying to us. As they converse with us they use, in much the same way as we do ourselves, a blend of vocal and body language spiced with a bit of direct mind-t~mind communication or telepathy, which is of course just as we communicate, one human being to another.

When we call our cats we use the soft diminutive, 'Puss, puss!' - not a bad imitation of the cat's affectionate 'Prrt!, prrt!' No wonder almost all cats everywhere respond to this call! When we are coaxing a cat we unconsciously imitate the cat's own coaxing call to her kittens.

Cats use their voices; not only do they answer us, but they usually have the sense to call us if they are stuck somewhere or shut in somewhere. What is more, they will often keep answering as we call so that we can be guided to them by the sound of their voices.

Cats are often such good conversationalists that it is possible to while away half a summer afternoon just talking to them, then wonder where on earth the time went to! They undoubtedly are also good listeners and detect every tone and nuance in our voices.

Tabitha, almost more than any cat, is an absolute sucker for admiration; she soaks it up like a sponge. She simply cannot resist the 'Oh - isn't she beautiful!' line, particularly if it is delivered in honeyed tones.

She may be lying there, apparently asleep, but get that tone in your voice, say those sweet words, and first one eye and then the other will open, and she will roll over on her back, front legs flung up in a gesture that appears the epitome of careless abandon but is, I am quite sure, calculated to a whisker's width; she will roll her head round, one large ear often turned under so that she has a curiously appealing look of being skew-wiff, and reply, 'prrt! I am beautiful, aren't I?'

It is much the same sound and much the same attitude that a mother cat adopts when she has kittens she wants admired. Tabitha, being a spayed cat, has only herself to show off, and this she does to perfection. There are all sorts of cat conversations; between cats, between cats and people, and between people about cats. These last, I have discovered, are likely to be both prolonged and involved. Shaggy-dog stories have nothing on cool-cat ones!

Get any group of cat lovers together and there will be no stopping them. Each will vie with the other to talk about his or her cat, and, quite unlike dog or horse people who tell stories boasting about the prowess and good training of their animals, cat people are likely to tell yarns that show the cat as the superior being - often getting the better, by rather devious means, of their human owners. I have noticed that cat people never mind telling stories against themselves if it shows their cat in a good light.

Cat language as such has not really been studied with any seriousness. A French naturalist, Dupont de Nemours, was laughed at by his eighteenth century contemporaries for his studies of animal language. He said: 'Those who utter sounds attach significance to them; their fellows do the same, and those sounds originally inspired by passion and repeated under similar recurrent circumstances, become the abiding expressions of the passions that gave rise to them.' A very true observation which applies, no doubt, equally well to human and cat language!

Chateaubriand was particularly interested in Dupont de Nemours' researches into cat language. One of the conclusions the latter came to was that the cat had a language that made use of the same vowel sounds as the dog, with the addition of six consonants - m,n,g,h,v and f. This gave the cat a greater number of 'words' than the dog.

The conversation of cats seems to have had a great fascination for French cat lovers of earlier centuries. The Abbé Galiani made a close study of his own cats, which he cut off from any communication with outside cats, and came to the following conclusion: 'I am sure there are more than twenty different inflections in the language of cats, and there really is a "tongue", for they always employ the same sound to express the same thing.

This is an observation which almost any observant cat lover would be able to make. But a nineteenth- century French professor, Leon Grimaldi, went even further and declared that in his opinion, 'Cats can talk as readily as human beings.' He claimed to have learned their language and to be able to converse with them. Cat language, the professor said, was more like modern Chinese than anything else and consisted of about 600 words. To prove his point he gave a vocabulary I wish I could get a hold of a copy!

But maybe it is as well we don't always know just what our cats are saying to us and about us. It might totally shatter any illusions we might have about our being the superior species!

Helen Winslow in her delightful book *Concerning Cats* published in 1900, has some enchanting stories to tell about conversations with her cats. One little story I particularly enjoy tells how when Pretty Lady, one of her earlier cats, had her first litter of kittens, she disposed of them all immediately, thinking that the best thing to do for the cat. Pretty Lady was so brokenhearted that she became really sick, and in desperation Helen Winslow went to a neighbour and begged an unwanted newborn kitten to give to her. Lady was delighted with her adopted son and looked after him devotedly. A couple of weeks later, Helen herself was ill. Lady came and looked for her in her room and as she stroked her soft coat Helen said to her, 'When you were sick I went and got you a kitten - can't you find me one?'

To her utter amazement the little cat trotted out of the room and away downstairs to return shortly afterwards with the kitten in her mouth, which she placed carefully by her mistress's neck. Then Helen records, 'She stood and looked at me as much as to say, "There, you can have him for a while. He cured me - I will share him with you"!'

Helen was ill in bed for three days and the kitten was kept with her all the time, being removed to the end of the bed for regular washing and suckling sessions, but for the rest of the time placed by her neck.

Pretty Lady seems to have been a particularly caring sort of cat - almost a feline nurse - for in her book Helen Winslow relates another delightful story about this cat's power both of caring and communicating.

She had just breakfasted and was reading her mail when the cat came trotting into the room making sounds which she described as, 'Denoting her dissatisfaction with something - somewhere'. She obviously wanted her mistress to follow her. She was so insistent that Helen finally got up and went after the cat into the hall where she met her sister coming down the stairs full of concern about another sister who was sick and in some pain.

Pretty Lady led the way up the stairs to this sister's room. When she had recovered she told them how the cat had sat on the bed talking to her in the same sort of soothing manner that she talked to her own kittens when the pain was at its worst, and how soothing she found it. When the pain was particularly bad Pretty Lady went downstairs to fetch further help.

There is of course a way we can converse with our cats: that is by mental telepathy, or ESP. To many people such an idea seems totally absurd: yet how often do they use this very means of communication in their daily lives with husbands, friends and children?

Animals use this means of communication a great deal. They think visually, not verbally as we do. That is, they 'see' pictures in their minds rather than 'hear' themselves saying something. If we can attain this skill - or rather, regain it, for undoubtedly this is the way babies and very young children think - then there is a good chance that our cats can pick up the pictures in our minds, even that we can pick up something of the visual thinking in their minds.

One person who claims to do this to an extraordinary degree is Beatrice Lydecker. More than that, she can 'look' into a body and know what is wrong with the animal and she can 'see' over great distances. These two gifts have enabled her to work with veterinarians and give them help and also to locate lost animals.

She says that animals know when you are receiving their thoughts and usually relax and generally evince pleasure. An exception to this was a cat who hid behind a flowerpot and from this safe vantage point tried to figure out why it could see its own thoughts (mental images) in her mind.

In her book *What The Animals Tell Me*, Beatrice Lydecker tells the story of a woman who asked her advice about her two cats. Formerly extremely affectionate, they had been distant, cool, and totally unaffectionate to her after the death of her husband. 'Thinking' to the cats by mental telepathy, Beatrice found they, too, were grieving and felt that no one understood their grief. When she relayed this to the widow she immediately went to great pains to give them both love and sympathy. She reported that they immediately reverted to their former affectionate selves.

I think there is a very good point here. When there is a death in the family the four-footed members of it are often completely forgotten. Cats perhaps even more so than dogs since because they are less emotional in their behaviour it is assumed that they do not feel - a quite wrong assumption as the above story illustrates.

Fred Kimball, the American psychic who holds sittings for domestic pets, says that cats are secretive and likely to be less communicative than dogs. But this of course does not mean that they feel any the less deeply.

There have been several well-authenticated cases of cats going to the graves of beloved owners. I was recently told of a cat who often sits on the grave of the dog who was her friend and companion for twelve years, from the time that they were both brought into the family as babies until the dog's death.

Cats, it seems, can sometimes be more sociable than the humans they live with. Bill Schul in his book *The Psychic Power of Animals* tells of a cat that was his next-door neighbour in Denver. Henry was a large black cat and his owner was a widower not disposed to much conversation. Henry apparently found this rather dull but remedied it by having a set schedule of visits to the neighbours. He called on Bill Schul at seven every morning and remained for about ten minutes. Checking with other neighbours he found that he was equally regular and punctual in his calls on them, appearing to know just when would be the most convenient time to call on each household! On Thursday nights however, he invariably attended a local auction rooms, taking up his seat on top of a filing cabinet where he could watch the proceedings.

A cat with a similar yearning for social life was Willie, who went every Monday night to watch a group of women play bingo!

Cats of course are just like people; some are socially minded, some are not. I have often noticed that when we have visitors it is always the same cats who appear and the same ones who are missing.

On one amusing occasion all our cats were very antisocial. John's sister, her husband and four young children all visited for an afternoon. For the whole time they were with us there was not a cat in sight; as we stood at the top of the drive waving them off, our large family of cats slowly reappeared from strategic hiding places and began to rub around our legs purring and talking to us. It was quite obvious they were saying something like, 'Well, thank goodness that lot have gone!' I might add that they were a non-cat family, so the children probably would not have treated the cats with proper respect. But I often wonder how they knew all that - and where they hid; obviously they were somewhere where they could view the car and the drive.

Tiny was always coolly polite to visitors but appeared to quite enjoy meeting people. Except on one occasion. Our regular vet had a new partner with the unfortunate name of Death. He was very annoyed if it was pronounced so and insisted that the syllables be split so that it was pronounced Dee-ath. He had been to visit one of the farm animals and came into the kitchen afterwards for a cup of coffee. Tiny took one shocked look and bolted beneath the small serving trolley in the corner where she peered out at him, bright odd eyes wide with horror.

He put it down to the fact that he was a vet and she could smell the surgery smell about him. Tactfully I agreed and forbore to point out that in spite of her rich acquaintanceship with vets, or perhaps because of it, she liked them and usually greeted them most politely. I always put her antisocial behaviour down to the name - she was taking no chances!

If you think that is far-fetched then consider that it has been estimated that cats can learn and understand more than a hundred words in the language of the person, or people, close to them. If that is so why should death not be one of them?

Gillette Grilbe, who did a study of cat language, decided that though cats can make sixty-three distinct sounds they understand many more.

Sixty-three is a lot of sounds, certainly to most people who think that all cats do is miaow and purr! Actually these sixty-three can be roughly divided into three major categories: The miaow, which as we know has a wide range of tones, the 'prrt!', which covers both purring and growling, and the yowl, which is quite different to the miaow and, as anyone who has ever been kept awake by courting or fighting cats can attest to, also has a wide range of distinct sounds.

The more we listen to our cats and note the connection between individual sounds and actions and circumstances, the more we will understand cat language, and the more we talk to our cats the more attentive they will be to our language and thus the greater the understanding between us - the better our conversations.

A common belief about cats is that they have unexpressive faces. This of course is totally incorrect. To the observant cat lover their faces are full of expression. This is revealed in many ways: the set of the ears, the lips (there can be no mistaking an angry feline snarl with lips drawn back to reveal sharp fangs), the whiskers, and of course the eyes. No animal, and that includes man himself, has such remarkable and expressive eyes as the cat: they can be wide with interest and excitement, half-closed in pleasure and relaxation or flashing in anger.

Like any other worthwhile exercise, learning to understand our cats and communicate with them means the expenditure of both time and effort. It also involves the use of our own five senses and study of the five senses of our feline friends.

Real understanding of our cats on this sensory level means not only greatly improved powers of communication but the possibility of deeper understanding on another plane - the psychic - through an awakening of our sixth sense, already highly developed in most cats. What richer reward could we hope for?

Chapter 16
The Soul of a Cat

The unfortunate thing about animal souls is that we do not often even ponder their existence until the time comes for them to leave the body. In the natural grief we feel at losing a beloved friend we ask, 'is this the end?'

I have never been able to understand the peculiar logic that states categorically that while man is immortal the animals are not. Like it or not, we all share the same life force, are all animals on the same planet. If one is snuffed out at death, then all are. Since 1 cannot subscribe to the latter view, chiefly on the grounds of economics (it would be so wasteful of experience, knowledge, of life itself), then I believe in immortality - in some form or another.

To think about the cat's soul only when it is dying seems rather selfish, as if we want it to be immortal for our sake, not for its own; so let's take a look at the evidence for 'something' - soul, spirit, eternal life force - call it what you will - in cats that are very much alive.

One definition of soul is 'that essential something,' the spark that makes an individual. Cats have this individuality to a marked degree. We can also assume that having clairvoyant powers - being psychic - is another manifestation of soul. Cats are thought by many people to be one of the most advanced of animals and a great many mediums not only have cats as companions but have them in the room with them when they are holding seances or giving private sittings, because they feel that the cat's own psychic powers make for success.

It is no idle speculation to say that the cat is a psychic animal. It has to be to survive. It is the whole nature of the cat to be a loner, to live and hunt on its own. Not only has the cat remarkable eyes and eyesight but very sensitive hearing, an acute sense of smell and a delicate sense of touch. Cats are made for total awareness and can respond instantly to the slightest stimuli. Much of this awareness is through the five senses, it is true, but they also have an uncannily accurate sense of time, an unbuilt clock.

It may be argued that the cat is not really psychic at all, but that she merely has five remarkably good senses which she uses to good account. To a certain extent this is so. It can also be said that we all - feline or human, psychic or not - store data recorded by our five senses in our subconscious mind for the conscious mind to draw on as and when required. But when a cat picks up a message about something that is happening hundreds, or even thousands, of miles away, or reaches a destination many miles distant to be reunited with a loved person, even though it has never been there before, then we are forced to assume that is using a sixth sense - PSI.

There are a great many cases of cats travelling long distances back to their old homes when a family move takes place. Because of this many people do not try to move cats believing, quite erroneously, that they are more attached to places than to people. Incredible though some of these journeys are, it is possible to assume there must be some logical and natural explanation for a cat finding its way back to a place it knows.

But how do you explain a cat travelling a vast distance, over completely unknown territory, to find its owners in a new home? Because there seems no logical explanation, this has been called 'PSI-Trailing'. One of the most documented cases is that of Sugar, a cream Persian belonging to Mr & Mrs Woods of Anderson, California.

On his retirement Mr Woods and his wife planned to move to Gage, in Oklahoma, to live on a farm. They knew from past experience that Sugar hated travelling by car, so they arranged to leave him with neighbours whom he knew and who liked him.

Over a year later, Sugar turned up at the Wood's farm in Oklahoma, well over 1000 miles away.

At first they did not believe it was him, but just a cat remarkably similar, however, Sugar had a slight deformity of the left hip joint, which never seemed to effect him and was only noticeable when he was being petted, when it could be felt under the hand. Mrs Woods was caressing the 'new' cat one day when her hand come on the unmistakably individual hip joint.

They immediately got in touch with the family in California where they had left Sugar and learned that he had walked out just three weeks after they left for Oklahoma. He had been travelling thirteen months to reach his family - but how did he know where they were?

In his book *The Psychic Power of Animals*, Bill Schul tells the story of another Persian who apparently knew when her mistress died, though one was in America, the other in England.

His next-door neighbour was boarding the cat for her mother who was on a visit to England. The cat and the woman had lived together in an apartment for four years and had never been separated in that time. However, after the first few days the cat adjusted happily to her new environment. A month later the cat refused food and just sat in a corner of the room mewing pitifully. Then it broke into a loud yowling. An hour later the phone rang to say that her mistress had died in England of a heart attack.

The only explanation for such happenings, if we dismiss coincidence, is some form of telepathy, some direct communication, plus a great love. Qualities which, in humans at any rate, we would say were evidence of the presence of soul. If in humans, then why not in cats?

Perhaps too when cats show an altruistic concern for others, cats or people, we could say that it is evidence of soul. I recently heard a remarkable story of a cat saving a human life. A man had accidentally shot himself while climbing a fence and was in danger of bleeding to death. Timmy, out on the prowl, found him, raced back home to his master whom he found in the sheds; shouting and miaowing, he literally tore at his legs then raced back in the direction he had come only to repeat the performance. Realising this behaviour was quite extraordinary the man got the message and followed the cat. As a result the injured man reached medical aid in time to save his life.

Anyone who has had much to do with cats over the years will have 'deathbed' stories to tell. I have never forgotten how my beloved Tiny died, sitting by the stove in her favourite cosy spot, purring as I stroked her. No injury, no sign of sickness. It was as if she were saying 'I'm going now; you don't really need me any more.' I grieved for her, and I missed her, but she was quite right: had she died when she and I were living alone it would have shattered my world. I loved her as much as ever, but I no longer needed her in my new life with a husband and child.

There have been the cats who have crawled home to die. Smokey, my father's beloved blue-and-white cat went missing. We searched and searched to no avail. A couple of days later he staggered into the house, through the kitchen where we were drinking morning coffee, up the hall and the long passage to my father's office at the front of the house to collapse on the mat by my father's chair at his desk and die, in the spot where he had spent so many of his waking hours.

There was another blue cat early in my marriage, a large and handsome tom who had reigned over the little harem of farm cats until he disappeared one day. Over the next two years I heard bits and pieces of news of him. He had, it seemed, taken up residence at another farm a mile or two away. Two years after he left I was amazed to see a blue wraith, a mere shadow of the splendid tom in his prime that I had last seen, dragging himself up the drive and towards the barns, his birthplace and former home. He had come back to die.

Later in time there was dear Tilly, who travelled across the world with us, she crawled into the kitchen of our Victorian home on the twins' eighth birthday (she herself was a fortnight younger than they were) from one of her rabbiting trips to die almost instantly, victim of 10:80 poison.

Seven years later her daughter Lottie died at twelve years after a prolonged and intermittent sickness. Lottie always slept with Max, my youngest son, then aged fifteen.

We knew that the end was very near so it was no surprise to me when he told me she was dead. What did surprise me was that he could give me the precise time to the minute.

'How do you know?' I asked

'She woke me up,' he told me, 'just before she died. I put the bedside light on and stroked her; then she died. 'I think' he added, 'that she woke me up to say goodbye.'

I was with Samantha, a much loved but rather strange little ginger-and-white cat when she died. Just as she was dying I seemed to be getting a message from her: it was almost as if she were saying, 'There'll be another one needing your help - one very like me'.

A few weeks later John, who had been lecturing the rest of the family on the need to be rational about our animals - not to increase the four-footed family and so on - returned home with a shy little tabby-and-white kitten. We called her Lucy and she turned out to be so like Samantha; a different colour certainly, but her disposition and temperament were the same. Lucy had been dumped outside the RSPCA kennels and when John went to do his stint of voluntary work she had been there a day or so, fed by kindly workers but not allowing herself to be caught. She ran up to John however and greeted him. Perhaps she was telling him that Samantha had sent her!

I suppose we all take as the most positive proof of the existence of the soul manifestations after death.

Dinky was a little grey-and-white cat, a sweet, gentle little thing, rather overshadowed by the more extrovert personalities in our animal family. Perhaps that is why she felt the need to linger around (we might notice a ghost) after her death. For some months after she died, I would open the door to what I thought was a mewing cat to find nothing there or, as sometimes happened, a misty blue-grey wraith that slipped past me as I stood there.

Many of my cat-loving friends have told me of similar things happening to them. One such cat was Abigail, a much loved Persian lady who was put to rest beneath the pink hibiscus where she loved to sun herself. Her human friend told me: 'The spot was just her burial place. Then, suddenly, she was there. As I went down the garden path I could feel her eyes following me through their slits. Sometimes I would even speak to her. For weeks this went on; then, suddenly again, she, was gone. She has not come back - she has gone on.

A friend of mine had a beautiful Siamese called Romeo; she had other cats and dogs, all dearly loved, but the relationship between her and the handsome Siamese was 'special'.

One night she put Romeo to sleep in the laundry with his special feline friend, she found it hard to leave him that night, but hovered over him in his basket telling him she loved him. Afterwards she told me how she wished she had listened more acutely to this 'feeling' and taken him, as she sometimes did, into her own bed. For she never saw him again.

At five o'clock in the morning her husband went to let the cats out, as he often did. Again some premonition caught her. She leapt out of bed crying, 'Don't!' But it was too late - Romeo had already slipped out into the darkness.

For several days her neighbour reported hearing sounds like a baby crying; there were no babies in the neighbourhood, but the cry of a Siamese cat can sound very like a baby's.

Frantic and tireless searching, endless calling yielded nothing. 'two nights later she was sitting in her daughter's room on the bed watching TV. Slowly the door opened a cat's width; Sam, Romeo's friend, pricked her ears as the hinges squeaked; slowly her head followed the distinct and clear cracking sound that moved from the open door round the foot of the bed. Romeo's 'ankles' used to make an odd crack as he walked, perhaps on account of his advancing years; the noise was well known in the family and was a joke between them.

Mother, daughter and cat followed the invisible sound as it came round towards them, and then back the other way. My friend told me that she was convinced he had come back to let her know his spirit was safe. Had she been alone at the time, she added, she would have found it hard to believe. From that moment on the strange 'crying' sound was heard no more.

Following Romeo's death Samantha and her mistress grew closer together, sharing their common loss. Sam, who hitherto had been aloof is now warmly affectionate, as if their shared sorrow bound them together.

I am indebted to Letty Gregory for the two stories about cats that follow. They are told in her own words.

For all the years they lived together, Carlotta slept alongside her mistress on the deep feather eiderdown for at least half of every night. It must be understood that Carlotta also had a busy cat life of her own and on good cat nights she would be late climbing the lattice outside the upstairs balcony and in through the window, which was always left half-open until she came in.

Carlotta died suddenly in her twelfth year. It was near dusk on a summer evening and she obviously didn't see the car as she returned from some errand across the street. Friend's grief must have been great as she dug a grave among the geraniums and laid Carlotta to rest. That night she found closing the window that she had always left ajar for Carlotta just too final, so she left it open as a sort of gesture. It was well past midnight and sleep still would not come. Suddenly she thought she heard the familiar sound of a cat climbing the lattice. Then there was a soft bounce and a thud onto the bed cover. She stretched out her hand. There was nothing there, but there was a hollow in the doona. She turned on the light to verify this. The depression that Carlotta always made was certainly there. After a while she shook her head severely, turned off the light and went to sleep, firmly lecturing herself on the danger of letting imagination take over when she was emotionally high. Before she knew it she was awake again, the well-advanced morning sun was streaming in over the room and the ache in her heart had eased.

She washed and put away Carlotta's bowls, telling herself that in time there would be another kitten, for a house is not a home without a cat, but there would be a little time of waiting - a dignified period of mourning. She then transplanted a pink azalea still in bloom to mark Carlotta's grave and hoped it would be compatible with the geraniums. That night she firmly closed the window as she retired. She lay awake for some hours but had just dropped off when she was awakened by a soft knocking on the window. It was bright moonlight. A perfect cat night, she thought as she scanned the balcony.

There was nothing there, but somehow she felt calmer when she had raised the sash a cat width. Before she could reach the other side of the bed there was that audible bounce and thud. She turned on the light and there again was that depression in the bedcover.

Friend did not try to explain anything to herself. From then on she accepted that Carlotta was still somehow close to her. She would even talk to her if she couldn't sleep and received great comfort from doing so. It was not a knowledge that she could share with other humans at this stage; in fact, it was many years later that she talked about it to me, so it was a secret commune that took place each night.

About three months later, as suddenly as she had physically gone out of Friend's life, Carlotta took leave in spirit. The 'happenings' just ceased to happen. Without warning or goodbye she was gone. Only her memory was left. Friend knew then that it was time to leave the window closed and to visit the local cat shelter for a kitten.

The second story is much sadder and closer to home, in that we knew this family well and the cat concerned was the firstborn of the first litter of one of our own beloved cats. It was presented in tiny, fluffy grey kittenhood to the slightly retarded daughter of friends and the two became quite inseparable. Then one sad day the little girl was killed, knocked down by a truck driven quite moderately in their very quiet side street. She had been retrieving a ball that had run down the steep driveway and lodged on the opposite footpath and had run right into the path of the heavy vehicle. The 'Fairy Princess', as her parents loved to call her, died instantly. There was nothing the distraught driver or her parents could do.

That night someone remembered Prince, as her pet had been named. He was now a very handsome, almost fully grown, silver-grey half Persian. They found him sulking in a corner.

No one could get near him. Gone was his placid nature and no more were his manners gracious. He glared and spat and growled and refused every offer of food. It was not the right time for battling with feline tantrums so he was left to his own devices while the family went on with its sad business of picking up the pieces of their lives and somehow putting it back together again minus the one, small, vital component that had been so much its hinge.

Next morning someone again remembered Prince and wondered if he'd changed his mood. He wasn't to be found. A little later his broken body was discovered stiff and cold on the roadway at the exact spot that the little girl had lain less than twenty-four hours earlier. He too had been a road victim. But it was such a quiet street. No-one had heard of an animal being hurt there before, much less a child. Furthermore, Prince, neutered early, had not been one to wander; in fact he would never venture beyond his own boundaries and would flee up the driveway in fear if someone as much as carried him beyond the front gate.

Did the 'Fairy Princess' actually call her Prince to be with her in whatever heavenly mansion is reserved for such special ones as she? Did Prince himself choose the place and mode of his death so that he too could pass quickly through the necessary portals? Not in this lifetime will we ever know these things. But they are facts to think about.

The cat - that supersensitive psychic of the animal world - figures in more stories of ghosts and supernatural animals than any other creature.

A case of a cat haunting a house was reported in the Journal of Psychical Research in May 1926. The house was an old one, built in the fifteenth century; it had at various times been a farmhouse and an inn, but in the mid 1920s when the ghostly cat was seen it was a private house. The cat was seen on several occasions, both by the occupants of the house and a friend staying with them. M described it as black, long-haired and walking with its tail carried on end. No one seemed to see its eyes as it always appeared either walking alongside them or away from them. The first time the owner saw it was when he noticed it trying to get into a cupboard. He went to stop it and was amazed that he appeared to be able to see through it. It moved away from the cupboard and he followed it through the dining-room doorway, across the hall, through the kitchen and into the pantry where it vanished completely.

He and his wife both saw the cat separately on various occasions but neither mentioned it to the other until a visitor remarked, 'I keep seeing a cat about the place which vanishes.

They came to the conclusion that it was a ghostly cat, and that it had probably been seen by other occupants of the house, who perhaps had not realised its spectral nature. It's attachment appeared to be to the house and not to the people.

The English magazine Prediction some years ago reported the story of a cat called Fingal. He was a remarkable cat, and much loved by his family. He was also, like most cats, a creature of very definite and precise habits. According to his owner, Celia Dale, 'He like to go out in the evening for about an hour, but would always return around nine o'clock when he would tap the French windows to come in.'

Shortly after he died the tapping on the window, around nine in the evening, was heard, so insistently that they would open the window, when the tapping would stop. On several occasions different members of the family were convinced they heard purring coming from Fingal's favourite yellow cushion. One afternoon a friend of the family came to visit and brought her Siamese cat with her. when the cat approached Fingal's cushion he arched his back in fright; then his eyes appeared to follow something moving towards the window. When the window was opened the cat visibly relaxed, to such an extent that he settled himself on the 'vacated' yellow cushion!

The story of another ghostly feline is told in Elliot O'Donnell's book *Animal Ghosts*.

Just after the turn of the century a Mrs Louise Marlowe was visiting a friend in the village of Congleton. One day during her stay the two women went out for a drive in the pony and trap when they saw, sitting on the top of a gate-post, a magnificent white cat. They were so taken with it that they stopped to stroke it, whereupon it leapt off the post and disappeared, much to their surprise as there was neither long grass or bushes to conceal it. Two days later they drove down the same road and saw it again; this time it appeared to 'melt away' as they approached. They stopped for afternoon tea at a cafe in the village and mentioned the disappearing cat to the waitress who only replied with a knowing smile. However, the woman at the next table overhearing them leaned over and remarked 'You have seen our local ghost!'

She went on to tell them that she herself had lived in the village more than fifty years and remembered the cat when it was alive. It had belonged to a Mrs Winge who, she said, had been quite devoted to it, and was heartbroken when it disappeared.

Mrs Winge was, however, both surprised and delighted when it reappeared miaowing at her door. She hurried to let it inside but no matter how much she coaxed it refused to enter.

This happened night after night and no matter how much she coaxed, the cat refused to come inside. Then one night it was a full moon and in the clear light the woman saw the ethereal quality of her beloved pet and watched it simply fade away.

After that she refused to answer the door to the cat's mewing and shortly afterwards left the district telling friends that though she was very fond of live cats she didn't like being visited by dead ones!

The cat - the woman telling the story continued - had been seen regularly in the village ever since.

Milton wrote: 'Millions of spiritual creatures walk the earth, unseen, both when we wake and when we sleep'.

Whether we look upon these creatures as spirits or ghosts depends very much on our own point of view - as indeed does whether we even admit their existence.

Harold Sharp, well-known in England as a spiritualist and medium, wrote in his delightful little book *Animals in the Spirit World* of a cat that appeared on a photograph after its death.

His sister had a smoky-black cat called Tammy that she loved dearly; she had four cats at the time but Tommy was much her favourite. One day he went missing. She advertised for him in the local paper and had many telephone calls from people claiming to have found him. She went to see them all - but none was Tammy. The last place she went to was a fish-and-chip shop. A - black cat had strayed in some days earlier but it was not Tommy. This cat was pure black, not smoky black, and had a sharp pointed face in direct contrast to Tommy's very broad, round one.

'I shall have to drown it then,' the owner of the shop told her, 'if it is not your cat. I don't want it!' His sister tried to prevail upon him to keep it but finally, as no doubt the man had hoped, she agreed to take it.

By now she had decided that Tommy must be dead, and indeed she never saw him alive again. She took the new cat home and fed him well and in time he grew into a beautiful cat. One day he was sitting on a seat in the garden; remarking how beautiful he looked she fetched her camera and took a photo. when it was developed, to her amazement there were two distinct cat faces, making it look as if the new cat, Blackie, was two headed; the second head was not his, but quite distinctly the broad face of the dead Tommy.

Delightful though these stories about the spirits of cats maybe, they do not prove the existence of a feline soul to the sceptic but merely that some people believe they have seen evidence of it. Does it matter? Our belief or disbelief will not alter things.

I feel myself to have a part of me that is truly 'me', that will go on when the body that is externally me has long crumbled to dust and ashes. If I can feel that for myself and for other people then why not for my small feline friends who have so much spark of individuality, so much - soul?

Cats' company has given me so much real happiness over this lifespan: I hope that I may be given the chance to enjoy it in the next!

FREE DETAILED CATALOGUE

A detailed illustrated catalogue is available on request, SAE or International Postal Coupon appreciated. Titles are available direct from Capall Bann, post free in the UK (cheque or PO with order) or from good bookshops and specialist outlets. Titles currently available include:

Animals, Mind Body Spirit & Folklore
Angels and Goddesses - Celtic Christianity & Paganism by Michael Howard
Arthur - The Legend Unveiled by C Johnson & E Lung
Auguries and Omens - The Magical Lore of Birds by Yvonne Aburrow
Book of the Veil The by Peter Paddon
Caer Sidhe - Celtic Astrology and Astronomy by Michael Bayley
Call of the Horned Piper by Nigel Jackson
Cats' Company by Ann Walker
Celtic Lore & Druidic Ritual by Rhiannon Ryall
Compleat Vampyre - The Vampyre Shaman: Werewolves & Witchery by Nigel Jackson
Crystal Clear - A Guide to Quartz Crystal by Jennifer Dent
Earth Dance - A Year of Pagan Rituals by Jan Brodie
Earth Harmony - Places of Power, Holiness and Healing by Nigel Pennick
Earth Magic by Margaret McArthur
Enchanted Forest - The Magical Lore of Trees by Yvonne Aburrow
Familiars - Animal Powers of Britain by Anna Franklin
Healing Homes by Jennifer Dent
Herbcraft - Shamanic & Ritual Use of Herbs by Susan Lavender & Anna Franklin
In Search of Herne the Hunter by Eric Fitch
Inner Space Workbook - Developing Counselling & Magical Skills Through the Tarot
Kecks, Keddles & Kesh by Michael Bayley
Living Tarot by Ann Walker
Magical Incenses and Perfumes by Jan Brodie
Magical Lore of Cats by Marion Davies
Magical Lore of Herbs by Marion Davies
Masks of Misrule - The Horned God & His Cult in Europe by Nigel Jackson
Mysteries of the Runes by Michael Howard
Oracle of Geomancy by Nigel Pennick
Patchwork of Magic by Julia Day
Pathworking - A Practical Book of Guided Meditations by Pete Jennings
Pickingill Papers - The Origins of Gardnerian Wicca by Michael Howard
Psychic Animals by Dennis Bardens
Psychic Self Defence - Real Solutions by Jan Brodie
Runic Astrology by Nigel Pennick
Sacred Animals by Gordon MacLellan
Sacred Grove - The Mysteries of the Forest by Yvonne Aburrow
Sacred Geometry by Nigel Pennick
Sacred Lore of Horses The by Marion Davies
Sacred Ring - Pagan Origins British Folk Festivals & Customs by Michael Howard
Seasonal Magic - Diary of a Village Witch by Paddy Slade
Secret Places of the Goddess by Philip Heselton
Talking to the Earth by Gordon Maclellan
Taming the Wolf - Full Moon Meditations by Steve Hounsome
The Goddess Year by Nigel Pennick & Helen Field
West Country Wicca by Rhiannon Ryall
Witches of Oz The by Matthew & Julia Phillips

Capall Bann is owned and run by people actively involved in many of the areas in which we publish. Our list is expanding rapidly so do contact us for details on the latest releases.

Capall Bann Publishing, Freshfields, Chieveley, Berks, RG20 8TF Tel 01635 46455